Windsor

Town and Castle

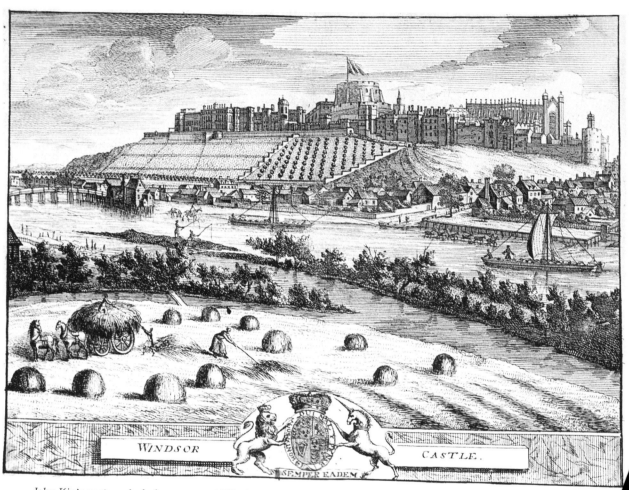

WINDSOR   SEMPER EADEM   CASTLE.

John Kip's portrayal of a busy scene at Windsor c. 1725. Boats transport goods along the Thames while people fish, or gather hay on the Eton side of the river.

Windsor
Town and Castle

Henry Farrar

PHILLIMORE

1990
Published by
PHILLIMORE & CO. LTD.
Shopwyke Hall, Chichester, Sussex

© Henry Farrar, 1990
ISBN 0 85033 746 1

Designed and typeset by
HURST VILLAGE PUBLISHING
Printed and bound in Great Britain by
BIDDLES LTD., Guilford, Surrey

*This book is dedicated
to all researchers, writers and artists
who have recorded Windsor's past*

By the same author:
The Book of Hurst
The Book of Pontefract
Selby: The First Three Hundred Million Years

Contents

	List of Illustrations	ix
	Acknowledgements for Illustrations	xii
	Acknowledgements	xiii
I	The Conqueror's Charter	1
II	Town and Forest	9
III	Building a College	17
IV	Rise and Fall	22
V	Elizabethan Tourists	29
VI	Downfall of a King	38
VII	A New Beginning	44
VIII	Change of Faith	54
IX	Joy and Sadness	63
X	No Expense Spared	72
XI	Beyond the Castle	79
XII	The Widow of Windsor	89
XIII	Victorian Inheritance	97
XIV	Windsor in Wartime	105
XV	Freedom of Windsor	112
	Bibliography	121
	Index	125

List of Illustrations

Frontispiece: John Kip's portrayal of a busy scene at Windsor *c.* 1725 ii
1. Windsor area prior to the Norman Conquest xiv
2. William the Conqueror (1066-87) 1
3. Windlass from a mid-13th-century manuscript and a Saxon ship 1
4. Old Windsor parish church 2
5. Excavations at Runnymede during the summer of 1989 3
6. King Ethelred (865-71) 4
7. Part of Gaimer's chronicle 4
8. Edward the Confessor accepts Earl Godwin's daughter as his Queen 4
9. Ancient font in Clewer parish church 5
10. King Henry I (1100-35) 6
11. King John (1199-1216) 6
12. Reconstruction of Windsor Castle under siege in 1216 7
13. King Henry III (1216-72) 8
14. Curfew Tower built in the 13th century 8
15. Hunting a stag with hounds 10
16. Women hunting rabbits 11
17. Edward I (1272-1307) 12
18. Prisoners being conducted to prison at the time of Edward IV 12
19. Jousting 13
20. Edward III (1327-77) who was born in Windsor 13
21. King Edward with King David of Scotland 14
22. King with his master builder 14
23. Windsor's Cross 15
24. Map of Medieval New Windsor 16
25. Henry VI (1422-61 & 1470-71) 17
26. Eton College from a print dated 1786 18
27. Henry VI's marriage to Margaret of Anjou 19
28. Richard Duke of York 19
29. Coronation of Edward IV, May 1461 20
30. Henry VI restored to the throne in 1470 21
31. Henry VI's tomb 21
32. Edward IV(1461-70 & 1471-83) 22
33. St George's Chapel 23
34. Henry VII (1485-1509) 24
35. Henry VIII's Gate 24
36. Henry VIII (1509-47) 25
37. Cardinal Wolsey's Chapel 25
38. Anne Boleyn 26

39. Butcher hanging from the Curfew Tower 26
40. Robert Testwood, Henry Filmer and Anthony Pearson being burnt 27
41. Dr. London and William Simonds riding backwards in Windsor 27
42. Prison in the base of the Curfew Tower 28
43. Ducking stool 28
44. Gibbet on the Berkshire/Surrey border 28
45. Queen Elizabeth (1558-1603) 29
46. The Duke of Wirtemberg 29
47. Windsor Castle at the time of Elizabeth I 30
48. Elizabeth I on tour in 1572 31
49. Water fountain 31
50. Bedstead dated 1593 32
51. Map of Windsor Forest 33
52. Queen Elizabeth being offered a knife while hunting 34
53. King James I (1603-25) 35
54. Windsor depicted by John Norden in 1607 36
55. Musketeer of James I 37
56. James I and his son Charles, November 1623 37
57. King Charles (1625-49) 38
58. Plague victims leaving London in 1630 38
59. Cavalier c. 1620 39
60. English archer c. 1634 39
61. Robert Devereux, Earl of Essex 40
62. Execution of Charles I, 30 January 1649 41
63. St George's Chapel 42
64. Oliver Cromwell 43
65. Small brass cannon given to Charles I 43
66. Charles II (1660-85) 44
67. Windsor parish church with maypole c. 1666 44
68. Charles II watching racing at Datchet in August 1682 45
69. Windsor parish church with King Edward III's Tower c. 1666 45
70. St George's Chapel with maypole and Curfew Tower 46
71. Upper Ward of Windsor Castle 47
72. St George's Hall during Garter dinner c. 1663 48
73. St George's Hall c. 1819 48
74. St George's Hall during a Garter dinner in Victoria's reign 48
75. Sir Christopher Wren 49
76. Charles II's statue 50
77. Horse and motor transport waits for customers below the Curfew Tower 51
78. Guildhall columns 52
79. Guildhall completed by Wren 53
80. James II (1685-88) 54
81. Princess Mary Beatrice of Modena 54
82. River Thames with Windsor Bridge and Curfew Tower 55
83. Queen Anne (1702-14) 56
84. Plan view of the garden in the Little Park 56
85. Queen Anne's bridge at Datchet c. 1780 57

86.	Windsor toll bridge *c.* 1760	58
87.	Datchet Lane.	59
88.	The Duchess of Portsmouth	60
89.	Windsor area surveyed by John Rocque in 1761	61
90.	Sheet Street in 1775	62
91.	Windsor Castle in 1805	62
92.	George III (1760-1820)	63
93.	Queen's Lodge	63
94.	Henry VIII's Gate *c.* 1780	64
95.	Thames Street lined with shops and houses on both sides	64
96.	Printing Office and Library, Castle Hill	66
97.	Datchet Bridge *c.* 1846	66
98.	The River Thames *c.* 1823	67
99.	Herschel's telescope in 1775	67
100.	The South Terrace with George III and children *c.* 1781	68
101.	Theatre Royal in about 1805	69
102.	Eton greets George III	70
103.	George III at Windsor in old age	71
104.	Chimney sweep and his young assistant	72
105.	Windsor Bridge in 1850	73
106.	Windsor parish church from Norden's map of 1607	74
107.	Windsor Castle in about 18103	74
108.	George IV (1820-30)	75
109.	Sir Jeffry Wyatville	75
110.	Round Tower prior to Wyatville's alterations	76
111.	Round Tower in Victoria's reign	76
112.	Upper Ward prior to alterations in the 1820s	77
113.	Apartments in Upper Ward in about 1840	77
114.	Copper Horse on Snow Hill in 1845	78
115.	The Long Walk from Snow Hill in 1840	78
116.	The Hall, Eton College	79
117.	Eton College seen from the Slough Road	80
118.	The first quadrangle, Eton College with Lupton's Tower	80
119.	Eton High Street	81
120.	The *Christopher Inn*, Eton	81
121.	The Long Chamber	82
122.	Seventeenth-century *Old Wells Inn* demolished in about 1880	83
123.	Windsor Forest *c.* 1801	84
124.	Windsor Forest	85
125.	Chinese Temple at Virginia Water in about 1840	87
126.	Map of Clewer	88
127.	Clewer parish church *c.* 1820	88
128.	Clewer mill	88
129.	Princess Victoria and the Duchess of Kent *c.* 1834	89
130.	Queen Victoria (1837-1901)	89
131.	Lower Ward "on Sunday afternoon"	90
132.	Upper Ward during the arrival of a state visitor	90

133.	Terrace gardens	91
134.	Christening of Prince Edward (later Edward VII) *c.* 1841	91
135.	Prince Albert	92
136.	Queen Victoria and Prince Albert with children	92
137.	Albert Memorial Chapel	93
138.	Edward, Prince of Wales, with his bride-to-be	94
139.	Mayor and Corporation of Windsor with Address of Welcome	94
140.	Queen Victoria's funeral procession	95
141.	Statue of Queen Victoria	96
142.	Queen Victoria and Prince Albert in a royal train	98
143.	South-Western station	99
144.	Great Western station	100
145.	Silver-gilt wine-cooler used at Royal Christening	101
146.	Harriet Monsell (Mother Monsell) at the age of 28	102
147.	Flooding	102
148.	Delivering coal to houses near the gas works during floods	103
149.	View of Windsor from the Great Western Railway in about 1910	105
150.	Church Street looking towards Henry VIII's Gate in about 1908	106
151.	Looking down Church Street towards the parish church	106
152.	Peascod Street in about 1908	107
153.	Second Life Guards on church parade in about 1912	107
154.	Caffyn's Corner	108
155.	Advertisement for the Royal Windsor Cycle Company	109
156.	Cycle shop in Peascod Street	109
157.	Marathon Race	110
158.	George V (1910-36) in 1917	111
159.	Cutting oats in the Great Park	113
160.	Trees felled in the Long Walk	114
161.	Replacement planting in Long Walk	114
162.	Windsor Bridge in 1989	115
163.	Map of Windsor area in 1990	116
164.	Tourists in the Lower Ward	118
165.	Peascod Street	119

Acknowledgements for Illustrations

The author would like to thank the following for permission to reproduce material in their possession as text illustrations. Her Majesty the Queen, Nos. 12, 87-88, 90, 102-103 and 129; British Library, Nos. 7 and 29; Clewer Parish Church Museum, Nos. 127-128 and 146; The Editor, Express Newspapers, Nos. 97 and 107; Guildhall Library, City of London, No. 142; Hulton Picture Company, Nos. 95 and 157; Imperial War Museum, No. 158; Judith Hunter, The Hon. Curator, Royal Borough Collection, Windsor, Nos. 47, 126 and 154; Museum of English Rural Life, Nos. 85, 159 and 161; Patrick Manley, 84, 93, 95, 114, 138-139, 142-145, 147-152, and 154-156; Southerans Ltd., 76, 111-113 and 131-134; Victoria and Albert Museum, Nos. 30 and 86.

Acknowledgements

My thanks for permission to quote extracts from publications covered by copyright go to: The Royal Archives for *Baroness Lehzen's Letters*; Webb Bower/Michael Joseph © Webb & Bower (Publishers) Limited 1982 for *The Illustrated Journeys of Celia Fiennes*; Local Heritage Books for the *Story of Windsor* by Maurice Bond; Phaidon Press Ltd. for *Windsor Castle* by Sir Owen Morshead; Weidenfeld & Nicolson for *Windsor Castle in the History of the Nation* by A. L. Rowse; J. M. Dent and Everyman's Library for Daniel Defoe's *A Tour Through the Whole Island of Great Britain*; Oxford University Press for *Jonathan Swift Journal to Stella* edited by Harold Williams; Methuen for *Edward the Confessor* by Frank Barlow; Macmillan Press Ltd. for *The Diary of John Evelyn* and *Highways and Byways in Berkshire* by J. E. Vincent; Jonathan Cape Ltd. for *Thomas Platter's Travels in England* translated by Clare Williams and *Letters From a Grandmother* edited by Gladys Scott Thomson; Barracuda Books Ltd. for *The Book of Windsor* by Raymond South, and the Editor for material from the *Windsor Express*.

In particular, my thanks go to all those publishers, authors, artists and photographers, whose work I have used but have not been able to credit.

I would like to express my warmest thanks to Judith Hunter, Raymond South, Patrick Manley, The Rev. Dennis Shaw and Knud Ravnkilde for their help in the preparation of this book.

Finally my thanks also go to the staff of the various libraries and Record Offices, Noel Osborne, Frances Mee, and the staff of Phillimore and Co., and to my wife Elizabeth.

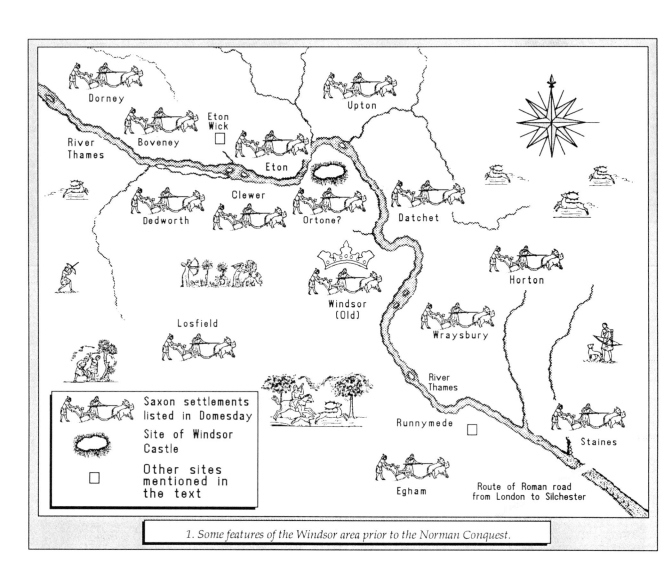

Dorney

Upton

Eton
Wick

River
Thames

Boveney

Eton

Clewer

Dedworth

Ortone?

Datchet

Horton

Windsor
(Old)

Losfield

Wraysbury

River
Thames

Saxon settlements
listed in Domesday

Site of Windsor
Castle

Other sites
mentioned in
the text

Runnymede

Staines

Egham

Route of Roman road
from London to Silchester

1. Some features of the Windsor area prior to the Norman Conquest.

I The Conqueror's Charter

"I have agreed for Windsor for the King's use."

When William the Conqueror defeated the Saxon army at Hastings, the area we generally call Windsor today was not much more than a chalk hill with a group of nearby settlements occupied by people who farmed the land, milled corn, and fished the river. When the Normans arrived, they were to make drastic changes.

Before the Norman Conquest Windsor was a large important community with a Royal palace and a community which depended on fishing, tending the forest and farming. By 1086, it was assessed as the third largest town in Berkshire. But it lay two miles south of today's Windsor Castle, at Old Windsor.

On the other side of the River Thames, Dorney, Upton, Datchet and Eton were Saxon manors which possessed eel fisheries. Eton also had two mills, and there was a third mill at Horton. Boveney supported its own priest, and Wraysbury was well established with two mills, four fisheries, and meadows which provided hay for the cattle of the Court. On the Windsor side of the river at Dedworth, a small number of people tended the meadows, ploughed the land, or worked woodland. Clewer was slightly larger with its own church and mill.

All these were well established manors before 1066 and many in the hands of the King. All have survived to become flourishing communities but some have lost much of their identity, swallowed up by an urban sprawl. Two other Saxon manors, Orton and Losfield, have virtually disappeared. Losfield was small, and possibly as its name suggests little more than clearings where pigs were kept, until it became encompassed within Windsor Forest. The location of Orton is less certain; its name implies that the people occupied a slope of land, and this, too, may very well have been enveloped as Windsor outgrew its Saxon bounds.

2. William the Conqueror (1066-87) enthroned, an illustration from an 11th-century manuscript.

3. It is generally accepted that the name Windsor originated from the Old English word windlesora *and means "river bank with a windlass". This illustration shows a windlass from a mid-13th-century manuscript and a Saxon ship.*

1

4. Old Windsor parish church, built in the 13th century and thought to be on the site of a Saxon building.

What is clear from the objects left behind by primitive man, is that the Thames Valley was occupied at a very early date. During the warmer periods of the Ice Ages, tribes of nomadic men, little more than ape-like creatures, hunted the area for small animals and birds, used primitive stone implements, and supplemented their diet with nuts and berries. They were forced to retreat to warmer areas as the climate became more hostile due to successive glacial phases.

When the ice finally receded, it left behind the main features of the landscape. These included the basis of the river system with flat, broad stretches of flood plain consisting mainly of sand and gravel, and a series of terraces formed as melting ice carved out channels, or deposited debris.

Man then returned and developed new skills at making tools. Eventually he learned the benefits of keeping domestic animals, and became adept at growing crops. He began to live in settled communities, and some traces of these sites have been found close to modern Windsor. One of the earliest, at Wraysbury, was occupied 3,500 years before the birth of Christ, and perhaps even much earlier. At varying periods different communities lived at Runnymede, near where the river is now crossed by the Staines by-pass, and to the north-west of Windsor at Eton Wick. All three sites have produced Neolithic pottery and late Bronze Age artifacts indicating that communities farmed the land, used arrow and axe heads shaped from flint, decorated themselves with jewellery, and lived in timber houses possibly having thatched roofs.

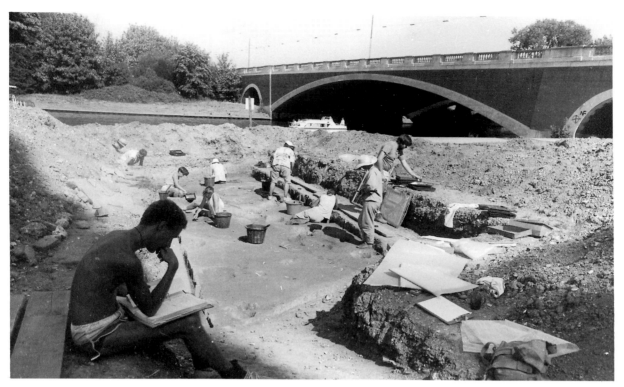

Approximately two thousand years ago the Romans spread across Europe and England became a frontier on the northern limits of their Empire. London evolved into an important centre from which they built a series of roads. One led to Silchester, after crossing the Thames just over two miles south-east of Old Windsor, at Staines. This and their use of the River Thames, brought activity to the area and scattered coins, pottery, a kiln, and two tile tombs, have been found near Windsor which date from this period.

5. Excavations at Runnymede during the summer of 1989 of a late Bronze Age settlement alongside the River Thames.

The Roman Empire collapsed, and by AD 410 all the Legions had departed. This left Britain open to further invasions by seafaring people who colonised the country and formed a multitude of independent kingdoms. Most were aggressive and endeavoured to dominate their neighbours. By the eighth century Old Windsor was a settlement at the eastern edge of Wessex, one of the largest and longest surviving kingdoms. The River Thames formed a boundary with Mercia, and to the south and east lay the kingdoms of Sussex and Essex. The inhabitants of Windsor must have been in constant danger as they lived in a border province during a very hostile time.

Early in the ninth century a considerable amount of land must have been cleared for growing cereals and a substantial mill had been built powered by water from the Thames. The mill was fed via a man-made channel, some three quarters of a mile long and 25 feet wide. The mill appears to have operated successfully until about the middle of the following century. Then the enterprise was abandoned and the waterway silted up.

6. *King Ethelred (865-71) who attacked the Danes at Reading.*

There is evidence that before the end of the ninth century, buildings at Old Windsor were damaged by fire. This may have been as a result of a raid by Vikings, who over a long period made several attacks in the neighbourhood. In 871 they established a fortified base at Reading, 16 miles to the west of Old Windsor. There they were attacked by an army commanded by Ethelred, King of the Wessex, and one chronicler wrote of "much slaughter on both sides". The fighting lasted a whole day, but the Saxons "could not stand before the fierce sally of the heathen men, who rushed upon them like wolves". They retreated and were pursued through the forest to marshy meadows at Whistley where they crossed the River Loddon. The chronicler Geoffrie Gaimer suggested that Ethelred was retreating to a base at Windsor. If so, his most direct line of retreat would have taken him across the Loddon at Whistley.

7. *Part of Gaimer's chronicle describing the Saxon retreat from Reading.* Windesoures *is mentioned at the end of the 11th line.*

When Alfred succeeded his brother to become King of Wessex (871-99), he paid the Danes an unspecified amount of Danegeld to buy peace and the Vikings withdrew to London. From there, however, they made occasional raids, burning and looting villages along the Thames.

Old Windsor came through this period to emerge as a settlement with a Royal palace used by King Edward the Confessor. He was a saintly king who, even before his birth, was said by St Peter to be destined for a life dedicated to Christianity. This prophecy came true for Edward the Confessor established a number of religious institutions and was said to have the power to perform miraculous cures. Later he was made a Saint.

The Confessor was crowned at Winchester on Easter Sunday, 1043. He is said to have possessed powers to heal the blind, a feat he carried out at Windsor. He also negotiated and granted a charter to Ramsey Abbey, and consecrated the new Abbot of St Augustine's, Canterbury, while staying at Windsor. Perhaps the greatest achievement during his 24-year reign was in founding St Peter's Abbey in Westminster, a monastery holding strong ties with Old Windsor.

8. *Edward the Confessor (1042-66) accepts Earl Godwin's daughter as his Queen.*

One chronicler described Edward the Confessor as, "a very proper figure of a man, of outstanding height and distinguished by his milk-white hair and beard, full face and rosy cheeks, and thin white hands with long translucent fingers". He was over sixty and near to death when Westminster Abbey was finally consecrated and he endowed the building with numerous gifts. Manors at Staines and Old Windsor formed part of a donation intended to provide funds to sustain the monks and ensure that they would pray for his soul.

Many of the English were still hostile to William, Duke of Normandy, when he was crowned in Westminster Abbey on 25 December 1066. He had defeated King Harold, Edward the Confessor's successor, at the Battle of Hastings. But the task of subduing much of the population still lay ahead.

All the Saxon landowners near Windsor were ejected from their manors which were then given to Norman lords. Westminster Abbey retained some of its estates, but a charter was drawn up for King William to acquire Old Windsor within a year of his coronation. "I have agreed for Windsor for the king's use", says the charter, "the place appearing proper and convenient for a royal retirement on account of the river and its nearness to the forest for hunting". Hunting was indeed close to the King's heart, but there was also a military reason. New castles, built to a revolutionary Norman design, were required to administer the country and protect knights and loyal followers. In the Parish of Clewer, a high chalk escarpment made an ideal site for such a fortress.

9. Ancient font in Clewer parish church.

Before the Battle at Hastings King Harold had held the manor of Clewer, and afterwards William awarded it to Ralf, who was one of the sons of Seifride. When the Conqueror realised the escarpment's value, he leased that part of the manor from Ralf for 12 shillings a year.

The site was particularly valuable as it offered extensive views over the surrounding countryside and could control shipping on the River Thames, then a major route between London and the heart of England. And there were vast areas of forest to the south and east, not only ideal for recreation and for satisfying the Norman lust for hunting, but also stocked with fine oaks and other trees to provide building materials.

The main feature of a Norman fortress was its high earthen mound, crowned by wooden walls and encircled with a defensive ditch. This lay at the centre of an open area used by the local population and their animals. This, too, needed the protection of an earthen wall and a wooden defensive stockade.

10. King Henry I (1100-35) who was the youngest son of William the Conqueror. After a 14th-century manuscript.

The Norman fortress built by the Conqueror at Windsor became part of a network of castles, centred on the Tower of London, spaced at about twenty-mile intervals across southern England at such places as Rochester, Hertford, Berkhampstead and Guildford, all built to keep the Anglo-Saxon population under control. Old Windsor continued in use by the Norman court as plans to consolidate the conquest were made.

During 1107 King Henry used it for his Easter Court when nobles from England and Normandy attended colourful events. But by Whitsuntide 1110, the King had decided Windsor's new fortress was a more suitable setting for his court. This established the castle's importance as a royal residence and ensured a new town would develop to serve its needs. Old Windsor began to decline as workers and traders were attracted to the new site which offered employment, opportunities to trade, and a measure of safety.

Twelve years later, the castle became the centre of great pageantry as King Henry married his second wife, Adeliza of Louvain. The Archbishop of Canterbury conducted the service, despite protests from the Bishop of Salisbury who claimed Windsor was in his diocese. The Archbishop, however, maintained that the King and Queen were his parishioners wherever they might be.

During the reign of Henry II, the Conqueror's grandson, stone replaced wooden walls to create a more substantial fortress. Only chalk and flint are found within easy reach of Windsor and these are not ideal materials for facing walls and towers. Chalk was used as filling and can still be seen in parts of the castle, particularly in the interior of the Curfew Tower, where the base served as a gaol. Because chalk is soft, prisoners were able to tunnel into the wall, but its thickness eventually defeated them.

Massive boulders were found on the heaths of Surrey within the old bounds of Windsor Forest and required great effort to transport and shape. They proved to be far more durable and impervious to weather and have outlasted more costly materials used in later building work. Lead for the roofs came from as far away as Cumberland.

King John is said to have loved Windsor Castle "above all others" and held several courts there; though sometimes with difficulty. He arrived at Christmas 1208-09 when "a most vehement and disastrous inundation of waters" covered the land.

The magnificence of Christmas celebrations at the time can be judged by the amount of provisions ordered to be sent to Windsor for the festivities in 1213. Twenty tuns of new wine for the household; four tuns of "best wine for the king's own use, that is to say, two of white and two of red wine; four hundred head of swine; twenty pigs; two thousand capons; fifty pounds of white bread; one hundred pounds of good and fresh almonds; one thousand yards of wove cloth to make table napkins and fifteen thousand herrings and other fish."

11. King John (1199-1216).

Two years later, King John chose Windsor for his refuge when England was under a threat of civil war. The barons resented his neglect of the country and excessive expenditure on the Crusades, and united against him. They were invited to come to Windsor and discuss the situation but they grew suspicious, and chose to meet the King at Runnymede instead. On 15 June, in an attempt to ease the situation, King John gave his seal to the Magna Carta. This charter was the forerunner of the Great Charter of the liberties of England whose main provision was that no freeman could be imprisoned or banished except by the law of the land.

However, the Runnymede charter did not settle the issues. King John revoked the agreement and during the following year, the barons enlisted the help of Philip-Augustus, King of France, in a bid to overthrow the monarchy. Philip's motive and reward was that the Crown of England would be given to Louis, his eldest son. Prince Louis landed at Sandwich and was well received by the barons in London and King John retreated to Winchester, and later to Bristol.

Most of the castles surrounding the capital were attacked. But Windsor was well garrisoned and in readiness when Count Nevers and Robert de Dreux laid siege. Their determined assaults made little impact on the walls. "They were long there, but did little" wrote a chronicler. Meanwhile King John took the opportunity to lay waste the unprotected estates of the barons, who were then forced to abandon the siege and eventually the whole campaign.

12. Reconstruction of Windsor Castle under siege in 1216.

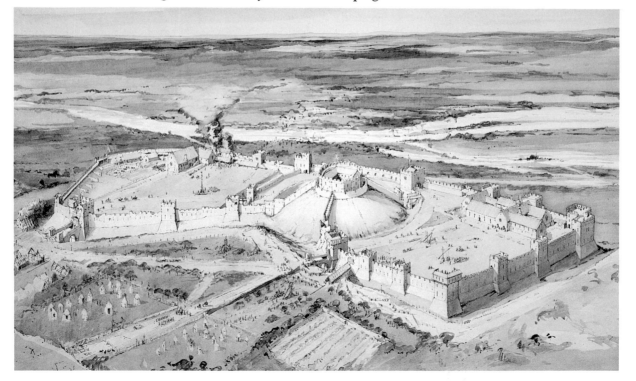

13. *King Henry III (1216-72).*

Military engineers learned that rounded towers offered the defenders a wider field of vision and were far stronger than traditional square towers. Any force applied to the exterior of a round tower, either by missile or explosion, forces wedge-shaped stones into the stonework and can add strength; whereas the same force applied to square stones in a flat wall may force them through and out the other side.

Henry III used this design when he initiated the building of new stone walls with towers covered by lead roofs to strengthen the castle defences. In the Lower Ward a chapel, measuring 70 by 28 feet, with a stone bell tower and dedicated to Edward the Confessor, was built. And perhaps most important was accommodation consisting of "another apartment for the queen's use, which shall be contiguous to the king's, and under the same roof" in the Upper Ward.

Queen Eleanor and many of Henry III's children lived at Windsor for long periods, even though the castle presented a threat to their health. Prince Edward (later Edward I) was said to have been in particular danger from the effluent caused by too many horses being kept in the castle. As a precaution horses were banned from being stabled there during the months of August and September. And as an added safeguard, when rainy weather arrived, all manure had to be removed.

Water was hauled up from deep wells within the castle's walls but, possibly realising the danger of contamination from such wells, Henry III ordered cisterns to be constructed to collect rainwater. He also provided money to buy ropes and buckets for the well in the Round Tower. This well descended through chalk to the level of the Thames 164 feet below and no doubt was intended for use during a siege when the garrison would use the keep as a refuge. Further attention was paid to hygiene by building a lavatory in the cloisters in the Lower Ward, supplied by water from a spring near the keep.

All Henry III's projects required large amounts of stone and timber and huge sums of money to pay masons, carpenters, plasterers, plumbers and decorators. Toward the end of his reign the exchequer was stretched and work held up for want of funds. But by then the castle had outgrown its wooden Norman keep and walls to become a substantial stone fortress with suitable accommodation for a monarch.

14. *Curfew Tower built in the 13th century.*

II Town and Forest

"... the Town became as it were destitute and despoiled, and the inhabitants also, poor and money-less, have ever since from day to day diminished, and continue so to do".

New Windsor developed on the two sites where the main activity was concentrated: alongside the river by the landing stage, and near the castle's main gate. Inevitably, life was dominated by the castle and the Crown appointed Windsor's officials who collected rents and taxes on behalf of the King. Windsor and Eton were joined by a wooden toll bridge, possibly built shortly after work began on the castle, but it was first mentioned in 1235 when five oaks were granted for its repair. Wood eventually rots and maintenance was often required which proved expensive. "The poor inhabitants" of Windsor petitioned King and Parliament in 1276 to allow the town to collect the tolls in order to provide money for the repair of the bridge, which had become so dilapidated "that no carriages or horses are able to pass over it without great damage". The town's officials were given the right to collect pontage, a toll paid by those who passed over the bridge and boats which sailed under.

Apart from tolls and taxes, other liabilities formed part of medieval life of the Royal town. In 1212 Windsor's bailiff, "along with faithful men of Windsor", was ordered to furnish men, horses, and arms to be ready to serve the King when and where required. But people did have rights too, as was demonstrated when townspeople complained to Henry III that Engelard de Cygony, Constable of the Castle, had done them injury by enclosing their pastures. The King responded and directed Hugh de Nevill and John Fitz Hugh to restore the land. Henry III was also obliged to respect the rights of those who lived alongside the south-west walls of the fortress when new defensive works were planned in 1230. He actually paid compensation to owners whose houses were demolished — a form of medieval compulsory purchase.

The scribes whose job it was to make records of taxes paid, transactions of land, or disputes in the Court, found it necessary by the 1200s to distinguish between Old and New Windsor. Those records which have survived provide examples of how trades and place names were used as a means of identification. Surnames were not in common use and some people utilised their profession, such as James the Glover, who was a bailiff in 1244, and Robert the Gardener, who held three houses beside the castle. The widow of Simon the Saddler became involved in a dispute over a house in Windsor with Hugh the Draper. Other people, some of them very important such as the Constable of the Castle, followed the Norman practice and used place names. William Fitz Walter, son of the first constable, was known as William of Windsor; Christina de Chalvey and Cugina de Burnham were sisters at St Peter's Hospital for "Leprous brethren and maidens". Two marks were paid to the king for a fishery at Boveney by William, son of Richard de Windsor. And Ivo, Reginald and Maurice were three men who also adopted the name Windsor.

The population of medieval Windsor probably numbered a thousand inhabitants. Some attended Windsor's parish church, dedicated to St John the Baptist, whilst others were still counted in the parish of Clewer and went to its older parish church. Trade was carried on in the market where people from the borough were authorised to hold stalls. Outsiders, like a number of Reading merchants who brought goods to sell in the market in 1261, were discouraged. James Glover, the bailiff, told the townsmen to assault the intruders, seize their property, and trample it in the mud.

A small community of Jews which had settled in Windsor by 1283 was also judged as unwelcome. Geoffrey de Pycheford, Constable of the Castle, gave instructions for them to be removed "without doing them injury".

15. Hunting a stag with hounds.

Windsor Forest was a large tract of land containing woods, heaths, moors, marshes, cultivated land and villages where Saxon kings had hunted for centuries. The Normans however brought new methods of forest management, better developed hunting skills, and introduced parks for keeping deer and warrens for rabbits and hares.

The Conqueror, and later his son Henry I, extended the bounds of Windsor Forest and kept the parks well stocked with animals. During the medieval period it covered a vast area and included parts of Surrey and all of east Berkshire almost to Hungerford. The whole area was subject to harsh forest laws with severe penalties for offenders. "He made large forests for deer" a chronicler wrote, "and enacted laws therewith, so that whoever killed a hart or a hind should be blinded ... As he forbade killing the deer, so also the boars; and he loved the tall stags as if he were their father. He also appointed concerning the hares, that they should go free."

Because these laws were particularly strict it was beneficial to live outside the forest's jurisdiction: consequently disputes over boundaries often arose. Most kings had their own ideas and included, or excluded, areas accordingly. A large portion of Surrey was released by Richard I, giving the inhabitants freedom from Forest Law, and he received 200 marks from the inhabitants in compensation. A large tract was disafforested by Henry III in 1227, the year he came of age, and new bounds were drawn up. By then the forest had been reduced in size with the western boundary not extending beyond the River Loddon, to the east of Reading.

Though the Crown held most of the parks in Windsor Forest, individual land-holders could obtain licences to create their own reserves for hunting — but often at a high price. These normally consisted of pasture and well wooded areas to provide covert for deer, fenced in by earth banks, ditches or wooden paling. The keeper was often provided with a lodge house at the edge of the park.

Early in the 12th century part of Windsor Forest was enclosed to form the Great Park. This became so well stocked with deer that, in 1202, 800 animals could be transferred to stock a new park at Langley.

16. Women hunting rabbits.

In 1246 Henry III built a "great Manor House" in the Great Park to provide more convenient accommodation when hunting. This became popular with later monarchs. In 1305 instructions were given for seven tuns of wine to be placed in the cellars of the King's house in the Park for the use of Edward I and his son. The cellars of the castle were provided with five tuns from the same shipment. Edward III enlarged the Great Park when more forest was incorporated. By then the manor house possessed its own chapel and a stud.

One of the forest's main assets lay in its provision of timber. This was a valuable crop in the days when most necessities of life were made of wood: walls, roofs, floors, doors, panelling, furniture, tools, containers, carriages, fences, bridges, carts and boats consumed large amounts. English ships protected the coast using wooden ships built from trees grown in the country's forests.

Probably since the 10th century the shires had been divided into "Hundreds", administrative areas which were thought originally to have contained one hundred families. Windsor Forest contained seven hundreds within its bounds and the Constable of Windsor Castle normally acted as keeper of the forest as well as Bailiff for these divisions. Under the Constable were rangers, foresters, verderers and regarders whose duties were to manage and protect the timber crop, preserve the King's peace, ensure the safety of wayfarers on their lawful business, and look after the royal vert and venison.

Over the centuries poaching was widespread and the forest made a good hiding place for bandits and robbers. In 1232 Gilbert and John de Starithe were arrested for taking greyhounds into the forest but after a trial received a pardon from King Henry III. Two years later the King was travelling between Windsor and Reading when Richard Siward and a group of armed men made an unsuccessful attempt to ambush him.

17. Edward I (1272-1307) who gave a charter to Windsor.

King Edward I held his Coronation feast at Windsor in 1275 and tents were erected in the Park for the occasion. Pageantry and grand tournaments were a feature of his reign when knights, many of them Crusaders, took part in jousts. They wore magnificent armour and rode horses fitted with richly embroidered saddles and bridles decorated with small bells. Edward I is best remembered for his charter of 1277. This gave (or possibly confirmed the gifts of an earlier charter) New Windsor the status of a Free Borough and released the town from a measure of control by the Crown, with authorisation to hold its own courts, collect taxes and form a guild of merchants to supervise crafts and trade. An annual tax of £30 — which was shortly afterwards reduced to £17 — was the amount paid to the Crown for these and other privileges.

From that date the borough could elect its own bailiff — as opposed to the royal appointee — and later charters gave Windsor opportunities to elect a mayor and aldermen. More recognition came early in the 14th century when Windsor sent representatives to Parliament. These privileges were reviewed from time to time by various monarchs and were not always endorsed with the same benefits.

King Edward's charter also established Berkshire's gaol at Windsor but many people in the county were not pleased with the arrangement. In 1314 an appeal was made for it to be moved, and it gave good reasons. "In the first place, the Town of Windsor is at the most remote part of the county, to the great grievance of those who ought to attend and common delivery ... and the Town is too small for providing victuals, by reason of which the inhabitants of the county avoid coming, except persons engaged to deliver the thieves; insomuch that the thieves derive great joy and encouragement in their evil doing ... Another point is, the commonalty of the Town of Windsor is so weak that the gaol cannot be sustained by the alms of the Town, whereby the prisoners die immediately, as well the innocent as the guilty, and those who have goods die before judgment is given, so that the king loses the goods and chattels of the felons, to the great damage of the crown ... The said gaol used to be at Wallingford, in the custody of the sheriff, to the great profit of the king and his crown. Whereof they pray, if it please him, that a remedy may be granted to them."

Prisoners had other dangers to contend with if they tried to escape. In 1309 a number broke out of the gaol and fled to the churchyard hoping to find sanctuary. They were recaptured by force of arms and a number killed and beheaded. It may have been such acts that caused King Edward II (1307-27) to concede to the request for the gaol to be moved to Reading.

18. Prisoners being conducted to prison at the time of Edward IV.

19. *Jousting.*

Natural disasters could be devastating, particularly to a population whose livelihood relied on agriculture. In 1340 all the wheat crop in Burnham was destroyed by a flood. This was followed by an infectious disease which killed most of the sheep, and the parishioners became so impoverished that more than three hundred acres of land lay uncultivated.

Weather takes no account of royalty and a great storm, which occurred on St David's Day 1251, caused severe damage and nearly cost the life of Queen Eleanor. A chimney fell and "the Queen and her children then was beaten down to dust, and the whole building shaken". In the Park "oaks were rent in sunder, and turned up by the roots, and much hurt done; as mills with the millers in them, sheepfolds, with their shepherds, and ploughman, and such as were going by the way were destroyed and beaten down."

Medieval people had a worse disaster to contend with when the Black Death spread throughout England in 1348 and is said to have halved the population. An Inquisition taken at Windsor 90 years later draws attention to the long-term results of such an epidemic: "... in the laps of many years, the said Town, by great mortality and pestilence at various times, was emptied and wasted, by reason of which the merchandise were withdrawn and the markets and fairs there greatly impaired, so that the Town became as it were destitute and despoiled, and the inhabitants also, poor and money-less, have ever since from day to day diminished, and continue so to do." This report caused Henry VI to reduce the borough's rent to £10.

Though people in the borough appear to have suffered severely in the 14th century, it was a period of growth in the castle and saw the birth of a fabulous ceremony which still flourishes.

20. *Edward III (1327-77) who was born in Windsor.*

Edward III, who had been born in Windsor and christened in St Edward's chapel, was proclaimed King of England at the age of 14 and became preoccupied with claims to the throne of France for most of his reign. He was later to became a great warrior and won battles at Crécy, Poitiers and Calais. To celebrate his victories Edward III founded the College of St George, and the Order of the Garter in 1348 — the same year that the Black Death broke out.

During his visits to Windsor elaborate tournaments were organised in the Park with joustings, feasts and other ceremonies. All this activity led to a need for more accommodation for College officials, courtiers and house guests.

A new building phase began, but as the plague took its toll labour became difficult to obtain. Orders were sent to all parts of the country to press workers into

21. King Edward with King David of Scotland who was imprisoned in Windsor Castle. A ransom of 100,000 crowns paid for his release helped finance work done to the castle.

service and send masons, carpenters, glaziers, plumbers and labourers to work for the King in Windsor. Those who refused were to be imprisoned. Only men employed on buildings for the Church, royal projects at Westminster, Dartford and the Tower of London, could be excused. This ability to press men into service continued well into the 19th century, as Tighe and Davis wrote in 1858. "The power to issue commissions for levying persons or things necessary for the king's service, was for many years a branch of the royal prerogative, and still exists in the impressment of seamen."

Agents were dispatched to scour England for materials: stone, wood, coal, lead, glass, iron and tiles. They were given power to commandeer transport to convey the materials, and coal was shipped from Durham to fuel furnaces and forges which produced intricate shapes in iron on the site. One shipment ran into a "mighty tempest" and part of the load was thrown overboard.

Extensive alterations were made to Edward the Confessor's Chapel before it was rededicated to Our Lady, St Edward and St George. Furniture, utensils, wall hangings, paintings and all kinds of decoration were purchased and brought to Windsor. William de Lindesay, "a carver of wooden images in London", was employed along with John, a canon of St Catherine's, who received payments for painting images. Large quantities of white and red lead, verdigris, vermilion, brown and blue, altogether about a hundredweight of colour and 22 gallons of oil were purchased together with 1,400 leaves of gold. The Lower Ward, the vast area to the west of the Round Tower, became almost entirely occupied by buildings to house College members and guests. A plan to enlarge the Upper Ward, the area to the west of the Round Tower, consisting of halls, chapel, royal apartments and gardens, was also put into action. This work did much to convert Windsor Castle from a fortress into a Royal Palace.

22. A king with his master builder.

Spending on construction fell considerably when Philippa, Edward III's plump and stolid Queen, died in the summer of 1369: "... she fell sick in the Castle of Windsor, the which sickness continued on her so long, that there was no remedy but death." They had been married 40 years but Edward, tall and dignified, soon acquired a mistress, Alice Perres, who was described as "that wanton baggage". Both she and her daughter Isabella are said to have slept with the King who eventually became infected with gonorrhoea. When King Edward died of a stroke in June 1377, Alice Perres robbed his body of jewellery. She took sufficient to live in comfort till she died in 1400.

23. Windsor's Cross.

Trackways, some of which had possibly been in use since the Saxon period, evolved into the main roads which lead to today's town. They were used to bring timber from the forest, goods from the landing stage, and by travellers who came via the ferry at Datchet and the Little Park (now Home Park), and those going on hunting expeditions into the forest. These tracks converged near the castle gate which became a meeting place. In 1380 a cross was placed at the intersection to provide a focal point for public gatherings and where proclamations could be read.

Some of the population no doubt benefited from employment and profited in trade as the castle and town expanded in the 14th century. But their fortunes do not appear to have endured for long. In 1438 an inquisition reported that the town had become depopulated, and profits from its courts, fair and market tolls, stallage and rents of assize had fallen by nearly two-thirds. A charter dated September 1465 also paints a gloomy picture. "These days the tenements in the Town aforesaid are much more ruinous than usual, and that the aforesaid Town and the inhabitants thereof are in a great part of the said Town reduced to great poverty, want, and distress."

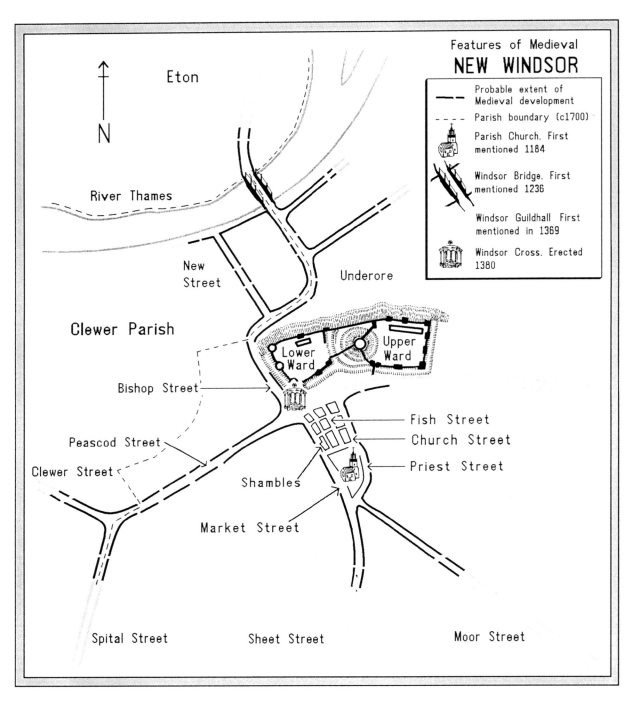

III Building a College

"... take as many masons, where so ever they may be found, as may be thought necessary for the said works".

The name suggests that before the Norman Conquest, Eton (translated as a village on an island) was a Saxon settlement whose inhabitants lived on land surrounded by meadows, marshland and water. Though the meadows often flooded they were fertile and bore rich crops.

The Saxon manor of Eton had been held by Queen Edith, wife of Edward the Confessor and daughter of Earl Godwin. Afterwards it became part of the holding of Walter Fitz Other, Constable of the Castle and Warden of all the Forests of Berkshire.

Eton's rural population lived within sight of Windsor Castle but if New Windsor owes its existence and growth to William the Conqueror and his son Henry, Eton owes its prominence and fame to King Henry VI. Henry had been born in Windsor Castle in December 1421 and succeeded to the throne only eight months later. His mother, Catherine of France, ensured that the baby king played his role and took him to preside over Parliament where he often "wailed and screamed" as the members tried to conduct their business.

25. Henry VI (1422-61 & 1470-71). Founder of Eton College.

One month before his eighth birthday Henry VI was crowned in Westminster Abbey. Through the inheritance from his father, who had won many victories over the French, in December 1431 he was also crowned King of France. His influence over the French was short-lived; under the leadership of Joan of Arc, they gradually won back most of the country. Little more than twenty years later, Calais and the Channel Islands were all that remained in English hands.

Though Henry VI was not a great military leader and was often judged as pathetic, weak, feeble and subject to attacks of insanity, he did achieve distinction by founding an institution which has played a vital role in British history, Eton College.

Some believe his motives were to satisfy his enthusiastic belief in his faith and discourage the followers of English religious reformers. This theory arises from a rule that Fellows had to swear to renounce the doctrines of John Wycliffe, Reginald Pewke, and other heretics on pain of perjury and expulsion.

Henry VI planned that the college should be run on similar lines to Winchester where boys who succeeded went on to Oxford. Eton boys were to progress to King's College, a new building in Cambridge.

A large labour force had to be recruited and Henry VI authorised "Robert Westerly, master mason of the work of our new College of Eton"; "John Beckeley, mason"; "John Smith, warden of masons" and "Robert Wheteley, warden of carpenters" to "take as many masons, where so ever they may be found, as may be thought necessary for the said works".

Men and materials arrived from many parts of England as Henry VI laid the foundation stone for the College Chapel on 3 July 1441. Stone was imported from Normandy at between 8s. and 9s. a ton. Less durable English stone came from Boughton, near Maidstone, at less than half the price. Flint arrived from Little Marlow and oyster-shells were purchased to "thrust in among the mortar, and key up the work". A huge number of bricks were fired in a kiln at Slough, and straw procured for the process also served as beds for the workers. The local forests at Easthampstead, Foliejon Park, Sunninghill and Cobham were unable to supply all the timber, so extra wood came from as far away as Newark. Carpenters were paid 6d. a day while labourers received 4d. Ale was available in local inns and alehouses for less than a farthing per pint.

Discipline, however, was strict. If a worker lost or broke anything, or was caught slacking, money was stopped out of his wages. Accounts show that 2d. was deducted "for playing" and "telling tales" while one worker was fined 6d. for spilling lime.

26. Eton College from a drawing dated 1786.

. King Henry had laid down exact measurements of all the buildings, though he often changed his mind which annoyed the workforce. Had his design been carried out for the chapel, Eton would have boasted a building only slightly smaller than that of St Paul's or York Minster. In the event his chapel was scaled down.

In the summer of 1442, Eton College Church was dedicated with "great festivity" and William Waynflete, no doubt the best man for the job,was persuaded to leave his post as Master of Winchester and administer Eton College. The buildings were formally opened in December the following year. One of the most important provisions laid down in the rules gave free instruction to an indefinite number of boys from any part of the world. They had to pay all their own living expenses, but tuition was free.

Henry VI richly endowed the college with property and gifts from the Duchy of Lancaster's estates to provide an income and ensure its future. Ten acres of land, "in a close called the Warde", were destined to become the famous playing fields. Even the Borough of Windsor contributed with a fishery on the river and the right of free passage over and under Windsor's bridge. Another gift provided "two tons of red Gascoigny wine, annually, for ever, to be delivered at the port of London". Apart from financial help, Henry VI gave Eton College wide powers. No person was allowed to lodge in the town without the Provost's consent; all houses were for the use of scholars and those connected with the college, and no other school was allowed to operate within a 10-mile radius.

Henry VI married Margaret, daughter of René, Duke of Anjou, and on 13 October she gave birth to a son. The arrival of Prince Edward seemingly assured the future of the Lancastrian dynasty but Richard, Duke of York, perceived it as a threat, thwarting his ambition to inherit the English Crown. Most of the country was drawn into the Duke's struggle for power as people took sides in the ensuing battles of the Wars of the Roses.

The Lancastrians were defeated at the Battle of Northampton in 1460 and Henry VI was captured and forced to recognise the Duke of York as his legal heir. Queen Margaret then raised another Lancastrian army and rekindled the war, determined to establish Prince Edward's right to the throne. In a battle at Wakefield the Duke of York was killed, with the result that Henry VI was freed from prison.

27. *Henry VI's marriage to Margaret of Anjou.*

28. *Richard Duke of York. From a statue which formerly stood on Welsh Bridge, Shrewsbury.*

Edward, the Duke of York's 19-year-old son, was left to revive the Yorkists' hopes and shortly afterwards the might of the two sides met on rising ground between Pontefract and York, near the village of Towton. Here the bloodiest battle ever fought on English soil was contested. Some reports say that more than 36,000 men were killed, hacked to death in a single day's fighting. It ended with the Lancastrians being routed and Henry and Margaret fleeing to Scotland.

Edward, Duke of York, was declared King by Parliament in March 1461 and crowned the following month in St Peter's, Westminster. But even these events failed to terminate the hostilities.

29. Coronation of Edward IV, May 1461.

The Wars of the Roses and subsequent shift of power could have brought an end to Henry VI's creation at Eton. Work on the college was halted while King Edward IV concentrated his efforts on St George's within the walls of Windsor Castle. He did not wish to foster the college across the river and confiscated some of its property in an attempt to dissolve the institution. But mainly through the efforts of William Westbury, who had been appointed Provost in 1447, the King's plans failed.

In the meantime, Queen Margaret refused to give in and brought about a revival to the Lancastrian hopes by gathering another army which was able to restore Henry VI to the throne in October 1470.

30. Henry VI restored to the throne in 1470.

Fighting however continued and Henry was again taken prisoner. Not long afterwards, Margaret's Lancastrian army suffered its final defeat at Tewkesbury. The Yorkists had had enough; Prince Edward was murdered and Margaret arrested and dispatched to the Tower. It is believed the King was stabbed to death, whilst praying in his cell, by Richard, Duke of Gloucester (later Richard III). Queen Margaret is said to have seen his body being carried past her cell window.

Every year, to mark the anniversary of Henry VI's death, representatives of Eton and King's College Cambridge place white roses and lilies in the cell where he died and on his tomb in St George's Chapel.

Henry VI's body was conveyed along the Thames under cover of darkness for burial in Chertsey Abbey. Later his body was moved to Windsor.

31. Drawing which shows how Henry VI's tomb was embellished when it first came to Windsor. Now it is represented by a marble slab.

IV Rise and Fall

"... a new pair of gallows was set up in the market place to hang all such as should come there from London".

Having effectively removed any serious opposition, Edward IV was restored to the throne in April 1471. Some impression of the splendid life at his Court in Windsor is given in the account of a visit by Lord Gruthuyse, an ambassador from Burgundy. Edward IV intended to impress his guest; he gave a splendid reception and presented the ambassador with a cup of gold, garnished with pearls and sapphires.

Next morning, Edward IV took the company hunting in the Little Park. The guest was given the King's horse to ride which he called "a right fiery hobby", and "a Royal crossbow, the string of silk, the case covered with velvet of the King's Colours". They only managed to kill one doe before lunch was taken in the lodge. Afterwards the party returned to the hunt and a record was kept of the details. "And by the Castle were found certain deer lying; some with greyhounds, and some run to death with buck hounds. There were slain half a dozen bucks, the which the King gave to the said Lord Gruthuyse. By that time it was near night, yet the King showed him his garden, and Vineyard of pleasure, and so turned into the Castle again, where they heard evensong in their chambers."

32. *Edward IV (1461-70 & 1471-83).*

After a banquet given by the Queen the party danced till nine o'clock and then followed a tour of the apartments. "And when the King and Queen, with all her ladies and gentlewomen, had shown him these chambers, they turned again to their own chambers, and left the said Lord Gruthuyse there, accompanied with my Lord Chamberlain, which despoiled him, and went both together to the bath ... And when they had been in their baths as long as was their pleasure, they had green ginger, divers syrups, sweets, and spicy wine, and then they went to bed."

Edward IV set about replacing St George's Chapel with a more spacious and magnificent building as a fitting venue for the Garter Ceremony. A survey revealed that the foundations were poor and walls crumbling. Richard Beauchamp, who became Bishop of Salisbury, was appointed surveyor and the old buildings were demolished to allow construction to begin.

By the time Edward IV died, in 1483, the building was sufficiently complete for his body to be brought from Westminster for burial, "with great funeral honour and heaviness of his people". The coffin was placed under a large stone within an arch at the north side of the altar. "Over this arch hung the king's coat of mail, gilt, covered over with crimson velvet ... richly embroidered with pearl and gold, interwoven with divers rubies." The tomb remained intact until October 1642 when the chapel was plundered by Captain Fogg, a Parliamentarian officer who removed the arms from the arch. In 1787, when the position of the grave had been forgotten, workmen chanced upon a lead coffin which contained the skeleton of Edward IV. It measured six foot three inches in height and had retained tufts of brown hair.

Edward IV's building activity had brought new life to Windsor. The wharf and river traffic must have been stretched to capacity handling construction materials, and the market traders and inns found new customers.

33. St George's Chapel. From a drawing by F. Mackenzie.

As St George's Chapel was completed, the building became renowned for its beauty and the quality of the craftsmanship, and its fame as a place of worship spread far beyond the small market town in which it stood. Many travellers and pilgrims regarded it as a shrine and came to pay homage. But above all, it was the scene where people of eminence were invited to be installed as Knights of the Garter.

One visitor, Philip, King of Castile, came unexpectedly in 1506 after his ship had been driven on to the Dorset coast by a gale. He was returning home having won a victory in the Low Countries and used the opportunity to make an unplanned visit to King Henry VII who was holding court at Windsor.

34. Henry VII (1485-1509).

Hearing the news, Henry gave instructions for all the gentry on the route to help Philip on his way and dispatched the Prince of Wales (later Henry VIII) to meet and accompany him to a site "a mile or more out of Windsor", where Henry VII would be waiting. The two Kings met and embraced before riding in procession, with trumpets sounding, up Peascod Street to the castle. Feasting, dancing and hunting parties were arranged to entertain Philip during his two-week visit.

Such was the friendship between the two kings that Philip was installed as a Knight of the Garter and the Treaty of Windsor, binding the two countries in an alliance, was agreed before the High Altar of St George's Chapel. The treaty came to an end with the Spanish Armada 82 years later but history was echoed in June 1989 when Her Majesty, Queen Elizabeth II, installed the King of Spain as an Extra Knight in the Order, thus confirming ancient friendships.

In the first year of his reign, King Henry VIII built the great gateway to Windsor Castle which gave the Lower Ward the impressive entrance used today. He was a large man and the gate which bears his name is appropriately massive. Two imposing towers are separated by an arch with holes above intended to be used to pour boiling oil on unwelcome visitors. Now all tourists to the castle pass safely through the arch and under Henry VIII's symbols which decorate the front: the portcullis, the fleur de lis and combined roses of Lancaster and Yorkshire.

35. Henry VIII's Gate.

King Henry VIII married his widowed sister-in-law, Catherine of Aragon, only two months after succeeding to the throne and shortly afterwards the entire court, which had often spent much of its time in Greenwich, moved to Windsor, bringing crowds of nobles and courtiers to the town. The resulting increase in the town's prosperity is reflected in the tax returns. One payment of £178 was higher than amounts paid by larger populations such as those at Plymouth and Winchester.

Henry VIII amused himself playing tennis, singing, dancing, writing ballads, playing music and hunting. "His Grace, every afternoon, when the weather is any thing fair, does ride forth on hawking or walks in the Park, and comes not in again till it be late in the evening."

The Garter Ceremonies were especially lavish and spectacular, with cavalcades passing along the streets of Eton and Windsor. On one occasion Henry VIII rode to Colnbrook and from there headed a procession of Dukes, Marquesses, Earls, Barons, Knights and noblemen, to Windsor Castle. Queen Catherine watched the cavalcade's early progression, then, while they proceeded through Upton to Eton, she and her ladies took the Datchet ferry to await their arrival, "where all they of the college stood along". The procession passed over the bridge to Thames Street and on entering the castle was received by the Dean and Canons at King Henry VIII's new gate.

In contrast to his lavish life style, Henry VIII is remembered at Eton for his meanness. The college spent £18 in entertainment and provided him with a sumptuous meal but were disappointed when he gave only 13s. 4d. to the church and £3 6s. 8d. for all the masters and pupils.

36. Henry VIII (1509-47).

Initially King Henry's marriage to Catherine was happy but of their six children only one, Mary, a sickly girl, survived and he was desperate for a male heir. When Queen Catherine reached an age when she was unlikely to bear more children Henry VIII became attracted to the charms of Anne Boleyn whom he saw sewing at a window in the Canons' Cloisters in the Lower Ward.

Divorce proceedings were long and protracted as Catherine bitterly contested the events. She had an ally in Cardinal Wolsey, a powerful statesman who also opposed the King's divorce.

Henry VII had appointed Wolsey as Chaplain to the King and Henry VIII created him Archbishop of York and Lord Chancellor. As Cardinal he attained a position more influential than any minister. He designed a tomb for himself in a new chapel at the eastern end of St George's which was to "exceed in magnificence that of King Henry VII", but the tomb remained unoccupied. Wolsey's downfall was precipitated by his opposition to Henry VIII's divorce and the King sacked him.

37. Cardinal Wolsey's Chapel at the east end of St George's Chapel.

38. Anne Boleyn.

In the meantime Anne Boleyn became pregnant and the separation was forced through. Henry VIII simply declared his marriage null and void and made arrangements to marry Anne Boleyn. In a glittering ceremony at Windsor she was created Marchioness of Pembroke, and her coronation hastily organised before she gave birth. Henry VIII's disappointment at the delivery of another daughter was so intense that he felt unable to attend the christening of the baby, Elizabeth.

Political and religious upheaval led Henry VIII to send investigators to the monasteries to obtain evidence of the corrupt practices allegedly indulged in by their inhabitants. With these testimonies he was able to denounce abbeys as immoral establishments and to drive out abbots and monks. The confiscation of the assets of these rich establishments greatly benefited the royal coffers. In the north, abbots and monks had allies who formed a band which soon attracted a large number of supporters. It became known as the Pilgrimage of Grace and included in its number many of the North's leading families. The Duke of Norfolk was dispatched to squash the uprising and assured its members that many of their complaints would be met if they disbanded. This they did, but the King reneged on his commitment and the leaders were hunted down and executed.

Discontent spread through Windsor, too. In 1536, a local priest was accused of siding with the revolution and, after a trial, led from the castle to be hung on a tree at the foot of Windsor Bridge. In his evidence he implicated a butcher who was also tried and found guilty. He was dragged across the Lower Ward and hung on a new set of gallows by the castle gate. It seems as if it was a deliberate policy to display the bodies in the two main areas of the town where they would have most effect and serve as a warning to shopkeepers, tradesmen and travellers. But the condemned men were not common criminals; they were ordinary people from the community and had died because of their faith. The authorities thought it prudent to post guards beside the gallows in case sympathisers tried to remove the bodies.

39. Butcher on display to the townspeople, hanging from scaffolding on the Curfew Tower.

In 1536, four years after her marriage to the King, Anne Boleyn was accused' of adultery and incest. The union was annulled and she was beheaded on Tower Hill by an executioner brought from Calais. Guns at the Tower announced the execution as Henry VIII left for Wolf Hall at Savernake in Wiltshire where Jane Seymour, who had served as maid of honour to both Catherine of Aragon and Anne Boleyn, discreetly awaited his arrival.

She became his third wife and eventually bore him a son. Celebrations were ordered but the excitement proved too much for Jane who became feverish and died 12 days after giving birth. Though Henry regarded Jane Seymour with great affection because she had borne a son, he could not bear to attend the funeral at Windsor. Princess Mary took his place and acted as chief mourner.

The rift between the Protestant community and the authorities widened when, seven years after the hangings, more people were persecuted at Windsor for their religious views. John Marbeck, an organist, and two lay clerks, Robert Bennet and Robert Testwood, were members of a Protestant group in St George's Chapel. Anthony Pearson was a popular local preacher who drew large crowds and Henry Filmer, a tailor and church warden, also sympathised with the cause. Their houses were broken into at night and books and papers taken as evidence. A number of them were arrested and Testwood, who was said to be suffering from gout and unable to walk, was among those bundled into jail. Trials followed in London and Windsor at which Filmer, Pearson and Testwood were sentenced to be burnt to death in public. They were led from the jail through the crowds, with Testwood hobbling along aided by crutches, to a meadow north of the castle where preparations had been made. As they were tied to the stake, some onlookers must have been outraged as they saw straw and brushwood added to the fire that soon engulfed the three martyrs.

40. Woodcut showing Robert Testwood, Henry Filmer and Anthony Pearson being burnt in front of Henry VIII's Windsor Castle.

Marbeck, Bennet, and some dissenters who were members of the King's household, were pardoned. Others were forced to ride on horseback, facing the horse's tail, through the streets of Windsor, Reading and Newbury, and be humiliated in the pillory.

Henry VIII married three more times before he died in January 1547. His embalmed body was conveyed from London to Windsor along a route purposely enlarged to make way for footmen who attended the huge coffin, with banners carried by the attendants. On each of the eight horses rode a child, dressed in symbolic robes. Even the streets in Windsor were specially cleaned by the Corporation for the funeral. "Canons and choristers stood ready to receive the body and begin the rite ... Crowds filled the wards and lined the streets. Not many persons in the crowd had seen a dead king brought to Windsor." The procession was so long that, as the hearse passed under Henry VIII's Gate, "the riders in the rear were fully three miles beyond the bridge". In accordance with his will, the King's body was placed next to that of Jane Seymour in St George's Chapel.

41. Dr. London and William Simonds riding backwards in the Market Place at Windsor after being found guilty of perjury.

42. *Prison in the base of the Curfew Tower. Stocks were not originally in the prison.*

43. *Ducking stool.*

44. *Gibbet on the Berkshire/Surrey border.*

A number of curious punishments had been devised over the centuries and most were carried out in Windsor. The pillory had been favoured because it had the advantage that the population could participate as offenders stood with their hand and heads held in a framework of wood. This allowed townspeople to ridicule the victims and pelt them with missiles. In the 13th century a new pillory was put up in Windsor Market Place where a good crowd could gather and be certain of a supply of rotten fruit. The town regularly contributed to the upkeep of such devices; Roger Printer was employed to build a new pillory in 1612 and £2 was paid to Godfrey Webb for the latest model in 1648. In the reign of Charles II, a Windsor attorney named Harris was convicted for "speaking seditious words of the King" and sentenced to stand in the pillory at Reading, Abingdon, Newbury and Windsor.

In 1515 the corporation paid 7s. 8d. for making a ducking stool in which unfortunate scolds were plunged into the river — not very pleasant in the middle of winter. Edward Umberfield received a payment to provide "Iron work about the ducking stool", and some time later three men were paid to move it. This may have been as a precaution against it being washed away by flooding. A flood did occur the following spring, and Mr. Frith accepted 2s. for retrieving part of a ducking stool from the river.

In 1636 a new whipping post was "set at the bridge foot". This was another form of punishment often reserved for women. Victims were no doubt securely held by new locks and chains provided by "widow Goring for the whipping post" in March 1668.

Gallows were fairly commonplace during the reign of Elizabeth I. To deter people from leaving the plague-ridden capital for Windsor, "a new pair of gallows was set up in the market place to hang all such as should come there from London". A gibbet was placed on the Surrey/Berkshire boundary between The Great Park and Bagshot. John Dean, a young lad of eight, was hanged in 1629 accused of setting fire to two out-houses belonging to *The Garter Inn*. Thomas Watkins was the last person executed by hanging in the Market Place. He paid the penalty "for the murder of Miss Hammersley's maid" in March 1764. His body was afterwards displayed hanging in chains from Watkins' Gibbet, which stood near the boundary of Old Windsor.

V Elizabethan Tourists

"There I beheld a bed of extraordinarily large proportions, very ornate, sixteen of my spans broad, and fourteen long, said to be King Henry VII's bed, and I never saw a bigger in my life".

45. *Queen Elizabeth (1558-1603).*

Foreign visitors, such as an aide who accompanied the Duke Friedrick of Wirtemberg on a visit to Windsor, had the impression that Elizabeth's England was "a paradise for women, a prison for servants, and a hell or purgatory for horses". Females were said to "have great liberty, and are almost the master, whilst the poor horses are worked very hard". The countryside around Windsor was described as "for the most part flat and sandy, and because few succeed in finding accommodation at an inn, they erect tents under which they sojourn, thus presenting the appearance of an encampment".

Princess Elizabeth was being held in confinement at Hatfield House when she received the news that her half-sister Mary was dead and that she had inherited the English throne. "This is the Lord's doing" she said, "and it is marvellous in our eyes."

The air in Windsor was regarded as the sweetest and purest within thirty miles of London and Queen Elizabeth was attracted to the town as a relief from the unwholesome streets of the capital. She arrived in the autumn of 1563 when London was suffering a severe outbreak of plague. The contemporary historian John Stow calculated that 20,136 people died of the plague in the city and its out-parishes that year. Elizabeth intended only a short visit to Windsor but she stayed all winter on the advice of the Marquis of Winchester. "I think her Majesty's best way, where her Highness now is in Windsor, if health there continue: although the house be cold, which may be helped with good fires."

Elizabeth put up with the cold building and made use of her time by learning languages under Roger Ascham. "I believe", he said, "that beside her perfect readiness in Latin, Italian, French and Spanish, she reads here now at Windsor more Greek every day than some Prebendary of this church doth read Latin in a whole week."

Children were invited to perform plays for her, while St George's Chapel earned a reputation for its music. Early in her reign Elizabeth decided that, "Whereas our Castle of Windsor has of old been well furnished with singing men and children, We, willing it should not be of less reputation in our days, but rather augmented and increased".

In 1592 the Duke of Wirtemberg attended a service in St George's and his secretary noted he "listened for more than an hour to the beautiful music ... The music, especially the organ, was exquisitely played; for at times you could hear

46. *The Duke of Wirtemberg.*

the sound of cornets, flutes, then fifes and other instruments; and there was likewise a little boy who sang so sweetly amongst it all, and threw such a charm over the music with his little tongue, that it was really wonderful to listen to him".

In 1572 a report by the clerk of the works described the terrace as being in very bad condition. The timber supporting the bank was so decayed that "it would not last another year". The Queen loved using the terrace and ensured that the necessary work was undertaken. It soon became known as Elizabeth's Terrace and, centuries later, her use of it had become legendary. Daniel Defoe in the 18th century wrote that Queen Elizabeth "usually walked for an hour every day before her dinner, if not hindered by windy weather, which she had a peculiar aversion to; for as to rainy weather, it would not always hinder her; but she rather loved to walk in a mild, calm rain, with an umbrella over her head."

47. Windsor Castle at the time of Elizabeth I. From Hoefnagle's Engraving in Braun's Civitates Orbis Terrarum.

Defoe walked across a lawn which he found was "kept as smooth as a carpet" and came across another example of Elizabeth's ingenuity. "Here is also a small seat, fit for one, or but two at the most, with a high back, and cover for the head, which turns so easily, the whole being fixed on a pin of iron, or brass, of strength sufficient, that the persons, who sit in it, may turn it from the wind, and which way soever the wind blows, or how hard soever, yet they may sit in a perfect tranquillity, and enjoy a complete calm."

Water had been brought to the castle in 1555 using pipes laid over a distance of five miles from Blackmore Park at Winkfield. The pipes were attached to a reservoir which fed to all parts of the castle and royal plumbers were appointed to maintain the system. This must have been a major technical achievement at the time and received lots of attention; "the water plenteously did rise 13 foot high" wrote one visitor.

48. Elizabeth I on tour
in 1572.

Touring the country to visit grand houses and stately homes became a popular trend in Elizabethan times. The Queen herself perpetuated the fashion by calling on wealthy families, often lodging with the occupants for long periods and causing them great expense and inconvenience. A number of travellers were attracted to Windsor for a tour of the castle. John Stow visited Windsor in 1572. He not only climbed the Hundred Steps, but also counted and measured them. "The ascent into which Castle upon the North part is by an hundred and twenty steps ... which stairs for the most part are seven inches". In the Lower Ward John Stow described the poor knights' dwellings as "in number thirteen, all of square stone, and each of them having a cellar, and hall, a chamber, a garret one above another, and a walk upon the top of their house which are leaded ... They have each of them a small garden plot before their houses fenced with a continual and decent wall running along their houses, and a common garden and conduit beside for public uses. The function of these poor knights is to pray for the prosperous estate of their prince and country, coming twice a day to the church". Stow described the Round Tower as "a mighty tower of diverse heights appointed for the governor's lodging, and joined thereonto a common hall, kitchen and other offices for them to eat together". In the Upper Ward John Stow made notes of "the princes halls, chambers, studios, wardrobes and galleries with stoves, baths and banqueting houses, and namely that great hall where St George's feast is kept, and celebrated".

When the Duke of Wirtemberg's secretary saw the castle he called it "a right royal and splendid structure, built, from its very foundation up to the roof, entirely of freestone, notwithstanding that this is not very often to be met with in this country, and cannot be procured without enormous and incalculable expense". Entering the Lower Ward he describes St George's Chapel as "a very beautiful and immensely large church, with a flat, even roof, covered with lead, as is common with all churches in this kingdom". He counted "seventeen poor knights, who have done good service in war and battle, either by sea or land, have their dwellings: they have further, as a remuneration and benefice, in addition to their lodgings, each a hundred crowns a year to spend, which is given by the Queen, together with a suit of clothes." The water fountain must have been working well as the party approached the Upper Ward — "the innermost court is quadrangular, of a bow-shot in length and width; in the midst of it is a curiously wrought fountain, all of lead, several fathoms high: in fact, all the roofs are covered entirely with lead, which induced his Highness [Duke of Wirtemberg] to cut his name in the lead upon the highest tower. After these, we were shown very beautiful royal bed-hangings and tapestries of gold and fine silk."

49. Water fountain which
stood at the centre of the
Quadrangle. From
Norden's map.

Paul Hentzner, another German visitor, viewed the castle in 1598 and found the baths and beds sufficiently novel to mention: "... there are worthy of notice here two bathing rooms, ceiled and wainscotted with looking glass; the chamber in which Henry VI was born; Queen Elizabeth's bed chamber, where is a table of red marble with white streaks; a gallery every where ornamented with emblems and figures; a chamber in which are the royal beds of Henry VII and his Queen, of Edward VI, of Henry VIII, and Anne Boleyn, all of them eleven feet square, and covered with quilts shining with gold and silver; Queen Elizabeth's bed, with curious coverings of embroidery, but not quite so long or large as the others."

50. Bedstead dated 1593.

Thomas Platter, a Swiss Protestant, also wrote his name in the lead on Round Tower and was shown the famous beds. "We then came to a large apartment full of royal beds, hung or tapestried with crimson velvet on which were embroidered in gold the garter and its motto. There I beheld a bed of extraordinarily large proportions, very ornate, sixteen of my spans broad, and fourteen long, said to be King Henry VII's bed, and I never saw a bigger in my life."

In 1600 Baron Waldstein of Moravia counted "5 beds, gilded and majestically rich, and spread with priceless coverlets" in one room; "one of them was 12 feet wide". And he saw how talented Queen Elizabeth had become at needlework, mentioning in particular "a beautifully embroidered cushion done by Queen Elizabeth herself in red and white silk" and "the Queen's couch were she sits when she wishes to consult privately with her ministers".

William Shakespeare is thought to have been Windsor's most celebrated visitor during this period. Attracted to the town by the Queen's love of the theatre, he walked the streets, saw the parks, stayed at an inn, and talked to townspeople while gathering background material for *The Merry Wives of Windsor*.

Paul Hentzner visited Eton and found that the town had retained its farming community and customs, along with its college. "... we happened to meet some country people celebrating their harvest-home; their last load of corn they crown with flowers, having besides an image richly dressed, by which perhaps they would signify Ceres; this they keep moving about, while men and women, men and maid servants, riding through the streets in the cart, shout as loud as they can till they arrive at the barn. The farmers here do not bind their corn in sheaves, as they do with us, but directly as they have reaped or mowed it, put it into carts, and convey it into their barns."

When Queen Elizabeth travelled, the cavalcade of luggage made an impressive sight. "... there commonly follow more than 300 carts laden with bag and baggage; for you must know that in England, besides coaches, they use no waggons for the goods, but have only two-wheeled carts, which however are so large that they carry quite as much as waggons, and as many as five or six strong horses draw them."

51. *Windsor Forest in 1550. From John Speed's map of Berkshire.*

52. Queen Elizabeth being offered a knife to make the final kill.

The Queen was a keen huntswoman and is said to have killed a "a great fat stag" with her own hands. Most guests, such as the Duke of Wirtemberg, were given the opportunity to hunt in the parks: "... there are upwards of sixty parks which are full of game of various kinds, and they are so contiguous, that in order to have a glorious and royal sport the animals can be driven off one enclosure into another, and so on; all which enclosures are encompassed by fences."

"And thus it happened: the huntsmen who had been ordered for the occasion, and who live in splendid separate lodges in these parks, made some capital sport for his Highness. In the first enclosure his Highness shot off the leg of a fallow-deer, and the dogs soon after caught the animal. In the second, they chased a stag for a long time backwards and forwards with particularly good hounds, over an extensive and delightful plain; at length his Highness shot in front with an English cross-bow, and this deer the dogs finally worried and caught. In the third, the greyhounds chased a deer, but much too soon, for they caught it directly, even before it could get out into the open plain".

Under Queen Elizabeth the fortunes of Windsor were restored. It is always a sign of prosperity when public works are carried out, and a flourish of activity in the Borough created many improvements during her reign. The streets, which in 1584 had become "noisome and foul by reason of the great and daily re-arrange and re-carriage" were to be "well and sufficiently paved or cause to be paved with good paving stones". New buildings were erected, including the market house in 1592, shown on Norden's map, and some timber-framed houses in Windsor today date from this period.

During Elizabeth's reign, wealthy citizens were endowing charities to enable such buildings as Franklyn's almshouses in Moor Street (now Park Street) to be established. This, and many other charitable gifts, perpetuated a tradition which led 19th-century guide books to point out that Windsor had more charitable institutions than many other boroughs.

Despite the lack of accommodation noted by the German visitor, Elizabethan Windsor had a substantial number of inns, alehouses and taverns which catered for people on tour and those attending Court. Taverns played an important role in the life of Tudor England and Andrea Trevisano, a Venetian ambassador who came to England in 1497, shows that they functioned very much like today's public houses. "Few people keep wine in their own houses, but buy it for the most part at a tavern, and when they mean to drink a great deal, they go to the tavern, and this is done not only by the men, but by the ladies of distinction. The deficiency of wine, however, is amply supplied by the abundance of ale and beer, to the use of which these people are become so habituated, that at an entertainment where there is plenty of wine, they will drink them in preference to it, and in great quantities."

The *Antelope* in Peascod Street; the *Crown* near the Hundred Steps; the *George, Rose, Cardinal's Hat, Cross Keys, King Harry* were only some of the more important establishments in Windsor. The *White Hart*, opposite the castle, was favoured by peers and knights while country gentlemen and those of lesser rank found the accommodation offered by the nearby *Garter* more suitable. Landlords were usually men of influence in the town and some served as members of Parliament, mayors or aldermen. They often sat at table to serve their guests personally. Trade, politics, news of Raleigh's exploits abroad and the future of the monarchy no doubt made topics for conversation.

Elizabeth died at the age of 69, having ruled for 45 years and reached a greater age than any of her predecessors. Her death came at three o'clock in the morning of Wednesday 24 March 1603 and a messenger was sent from Richmond Palace to take the news to King James in Scotland that he had inherited the English crown.

James I came to Windsor in the summer of that year and all was not well between the two nations as Sir Dudley Carlton discovered. "The King and Queen, and the Prince and Princess, came to this place on Thursday last, and brought with them a marvellous great Court both of Lords and Ladies; besides a great number that were here settled to receive them. Here was some squaring at first between our English and Scottish Lords, for lodging, and such other petty quarrels; but all is past over in peace." Queen Anne is said to have remarked, "so many great men did so little for themselves".

King James was a passionate hunter and inheriting the well-stocked parks at Windsor pleased him beyond measure. He was soon in the forest galloping behind the hounds in pursuit of deer. When a stag was brought down, he ran up to it to cut its throat and ripped open the belly. Often he would wallow in the animal's blood and daub it over his companions.

King James' administration of the parks proved to be less tolerant than that practised by Elizabeth. During her reign regulations had been relaxed and visitors were drawn to the Little Park to see Herne's Oak and sites of other scenes portrayed in Shakespeare's *Merry Wives of Windsor*. Townspeople had become accustomed to shooting hares or rabbits and collecting firewood in the parks and forest but this annoyed the King. He too was fond of rabbit hunting and did not wish to be observed by the crowds, and did all he could to prevent intruders entering the forest.

He employed John Norden to produce detailed maps showing parks and forest and closed off large areas to the public, including Cranborne Chase and the Little Park, which had access leading directly from the Market Place. Old forest laws were re-introduced with instructions to local magistrates that they must be enforced. But the people regarded the parks and forest as a public domain over which they had common rights, and few juries had the stomach to endorse the archaic laws.

53. King James (1603-25).

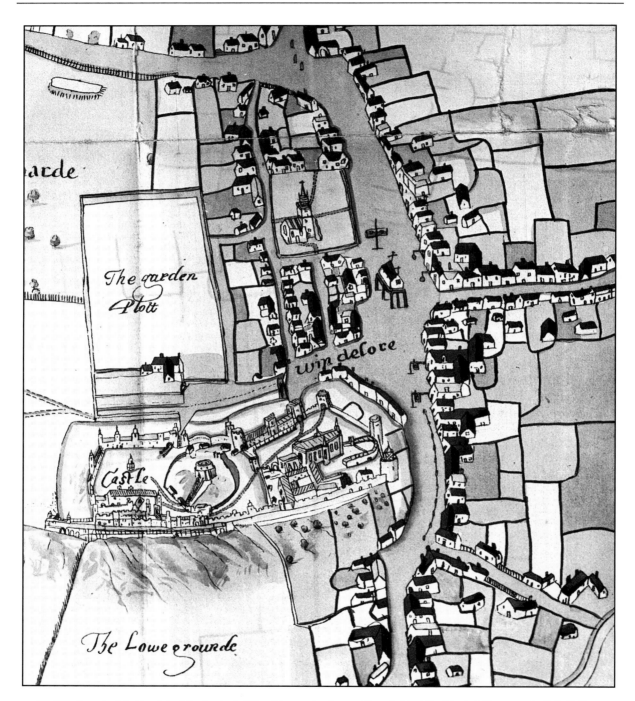

The labels on the map read: arde, The garden Plott, wjndelore, Castle, The Lowe grounde

54. *Windsor depicted by John Norden in 1607, with an extra large pillory behind the Market House or Guildhall. Just outside the castle, close to the walls, are houses which lined Thames Street. Many of them remained until the mid-19th century when they were demolished. On the other side of the road are two inn signs for the* White Hart *and the* Garter.

One day while hunting, King James was approached by a deputation from the town led by John Wikes, the mayor. They complained about the living of the vicar, the much respected John Martin, which was not sufficient to maintain his livelihood. King James seized the opportunity to put his own grievances to the deputation. He asked the mayor, "Why then do you vex me by permitting and suffering your poor to cut down and carry away my woods out of my parks and grounds?" Before riding off he commanded the mayor to have all offenders whipped.

Troops were used to clear the forest of intruders and old feelings of bitterness between the town and castle revived. Incidents of poaching and rioting increased, not only by the poor who were the prime sufferers, but also by men of means. Two wealthy citizens named Richbell and Buckeridge were caught and tried for killing deer. Buckeridge admitted he might have killed deer in the past and a witness swore he had buried a deer-skin belonging to Buckeridge. There seemed little doubt about the men's guilt; even so the court ruled that they were not guilty. In 1623 a Windsor man was not so lucky. He was caught trespassing in the forest stealing wood and so was severely beaten by the keepers that he died from his wounds.

55. Musketeer of James I.

56. James I and his son Charles (later Charles I) entertaining the Spanish Ambassador in November 1623.

VI Downfall of a King

"... in ten days from a height of greatness that his enemies feared, to such a lowness, that his own servants durst hardly avow the waiting of him".

As the result of a plague in 1603, a pest-house was built in Sheet Street and money was raised by the town to provide for the inmates and to keep the building clean. Windsor's streets were littered with rubbish, not the plastic and paper we get today but rotting vegetation, toxic animal waste and decaying carcases. In January 1635 a court ruled that any person who "do permit or suffer his hogs or pigs, or hog or pig to go abroad loose in the market place or any of the streets or lanes or to go un-ringed in any the commons, wastes, or common fields" was to be fined 12d. for every animal. The 17th-century equivalent of a dustman, "a sufficient scavenger for carrying away of such dust or other rubbish", was appointed by the mayor in an attempt to clean up the borough.

The town's water supply also received attention; Richard Michener was paid £4 for digging a new well at the south end of the Market House in 1637. Wells could be a danger to the public, however, not simply by supplying foul water, but because people fell in. Thomas Chermild erected posts and railings around the well in Moor Street in 1637 and two years later Thomas Sherwell did the same to a well in Pound Street. All this work may have been promoted in an attempt to overcome the recurrence of plagues which affected the town in James I's reign. Outbreaks occurred in 1624 and in the following year when Charles I succeeded his father.

57. King Charles (1625-49).

58. Plague victims leaving London in 1630.

During the first summer when Charles and his Queen were in residence, "there died two of the sickness at Windsor in a house where the Queen's priests were lodged". The castle gates were locked and the Royal party departed.

The Market Cross had been allowed to decay and what remained was ready to fall down when, in 1635, Dr. Godfrey Goodman, Canon of St George's and Bishop of Gloucester, decided it should be rebuilt. But his plan caused a controversy between the Puritan and High Church factions. Instead of rebuilding the traditional cross, he adorned the new structure with scenes from the crucifixion and topped it with a symbolic cross.

Francis Jones, the Mayor, protested to the Bishop and this was followed by a petition of complaint to Charles I asking for the crucifix to be removed. He rejected the petition and thus escalated the bad feelings between town and castle initiated in his father's reign. Early in 1642 indignant burgesses were said to have pulled the cross down but, by then, Charles I had other problems to occupy his mind. Parliament, and much of the country, had became hostile to his form of government and powerful men were plotting his downfall.

59. *Cavalier of 1620.*

In January Charles I entered the House of Commons to arrest five of its members acting against him. Warned of his approach, they had escaped by boat into the city. "Well, I see all the birds are flown, I do expect from you that you shall send them unto me as soon as they return hither", he told the gathering.

Parliament had no intention of surrendering the men who returned to the House in triumph. Sensing danger, Charles fled to Windsor where he and his family would be "more secure from any sudden popular attempt".

Unrest was widespread. On 14 January, Mr. Bagshaw of Windsor informed the House of Commons that, during the previous evening as he travelled to Windsor, he saw "several troops of horse" and "a waggon laden with ammunition". He talked to people in Windsor who told him "there were about four hundred horse in the town, and about some forty officers".

Parliament expressed its concern in a letter to the House of Lords, suggesting that "whosoever shall raise forces at this time, without consent in Parliament, may be declared enemies and disturbers of the Peace of the Kingdom ...". They urged that a message be sent "... to acquaint his Majesty, that both Houses of Parliament will be very careful of the public peace; and that they do hold it against the Law any such forces should be so levied; and that the authority of Parliament, and power of the Kingdom, shall be employed to suppress them."

Throughout the winter rioting took place at towns and villages in Windsor Forest. Fences were pulled down and deer killed or allowed to run wild. Commissioners were appointed to re-establish the forest's bounds while Sheriffs and Justices of the Peace were ordered to "repress all riots or unlawful hunting of the deer".

In February, Lord Holland informed the House of Lords "of the great destruction and killing of His Majesty's deer in the Forest of Windsor, especially in the New Lodge, where the People of the County, in a riotous and tumultuous manner, have lately killed a hundred of His Majesty's fallow deer, and beside red deer, and do threaten to pull down the pales about the said lodge".

Realising there could be more serious consequences of his unpopularity, Charles left Windsor for York to be near his massive supply of armaments in

60. *English archer of 1634.*

store at Hull. Lord Clarendon, who followed Charles I to Yorkshire, made this assessment of the King's unpopularity: "... in ten days from a height of greatness that his enemies feared, to such a lowness, that his own servants durst hardly avow the waiting of him".

Many who staffed the castle were local people and a tremendous pressure must have been put on their loyalty. Family quarrels and arguments in the inns would have taken place over which side to support as Civil War became inevitable. Parliament formed a Committee for the Defence of the Kingdom, and the borough contributed money to help its cause.

In October, Parliament anticipated the King's return to Windsor and appointed Colonel Venn to command the "troops of Dragoons and Volunteers, some of which are arrived already at Windsor" and take possession of the castle. Prince Rupert, leading a group of royalist troops, made an attempt to regain the fortress when "five pieces or Ordnance" were set up in the grounds of Eton college and bombarded Windsor: "... mightily battered and ruined, and the inhabitants very much damnified", said one report. But the attack was easily repulsed.

61. Robert Devereux, Earl of Essex, who received command of the Parliamentary amy in July 1642. Pictured at Windsor with the Castle on the left.

During the winter of 1642-43 the King's forces established bases at Reading, Abingdon and Oxford, while Windsor became the headquarters of the Parliamentarian Army. Troopers looted St George's, smashed down the door to the college treasury and took the valuable plate, much of it assembled less than three years earlier. The House of Lords sent a letter to Colonel Venn in the hope of protecting the college's valuables: "... take care that there be no disorders and disturbances made in the Chapel at Windsor; and that the evidences, registers, monuments there, and all things that belong to the Order of the Garter, may be preserved without any defacing". How much notice was taken of the letter is difficult to say. Delicate ironwork, the west window and much carved wood and stone did survive. However, Cardinal Wolsey's chapel was used as a magazine, some monuments, furniture and windows were smashed, the organ was defaced and valuable plate melted down to make coins and sent to Fairfax who was fighting for Parliament in the North.

Thousands of troops were recruited by Parliament and assembled·for training in Windsor. Accommodation was short and many were billeted at inns and private homes. The troops were responsible for paying for their own accommodation but as their wages were often months in arrears, it is unlikely to have added much to the town's income. During the winter of 1644-45, Sir Thomas Fairfax, who became commander-in-chief of the Parliamentarian troops, arrived to take charge of the "new model" army. Cromwell came to inspect the huge garrison before the troops left for campaigns in the west.

Defeated and humiliated, King Charles returned to Windsor for a short visit in July 1647. He was not yet a prisoner and as a mark of respect the town bells were rung. The sound may have gladdened the hearts of captives in the castle's cells, many of whom were personal friends of the King and loyal supporters. Attempts were made to negotiate an end to the fighting but they proved fruitless and the Civil War continued.

In September Scottish prisoners in the castle had become so numerous that the House of Commons was informed "of four barges full of Scots prisoners, that came from Windsor for Gravesend" who had been put into ships for transportation.

Leading Parliamentarian officers met in the town to make the fatal resolution that "the King should be prosecuted for his life as a criminal person". He was by then a prisoner and with a large escort bought back to Windsor just before Christmas 1648. The inhabitants braved the cold wet weather to line the Bagshot road for the captive's return. Shouts of "God bless your majesty, and send you long to reign" came from the people as the procession headed for the castle. The atmosphere was such that during the evening fighting broke out in the public houses and troops turned out to restore order. Many civilians were injured, others arrested, and three persons killed before the troops cleared the streets. "Terrible and bloody news from Windsor since the bringing in of the king's majesty", wrote a reporter; "... a dangerous fight on Saturday last, between the Parliament's forces and the Royalists, who, by a strange design and unheard of stratagem, would have rescued the king from the power of the army."

The garrison was increased and Charles was given "his usual bed-chamber" with freedom to "walk where and when he pleased, within the castle". He spent Christmas Day in a new suit of clothes but was denied "mince pies and plum porridge". Charles I remained cheerful as his trial was arranged. "He hears of the preparations to bring him to trial, and seems to be well satisfied for what follows." On 30 January the King was beheaded in Westminster.

62. Execution of Charles I, 30 January 1648 (old calendar).

63. St George's Chapel.
From a drawing by
J. W. Alexander.

Parliament agreed that Charles's body "should be buried at Windsor in a decent manner, provided that the whole expense should not exceed five hundred pounds". After laying in public view the corpse was embalmed and put into a lead coffin for transportation to Windsor where arrangements were made to receive the coffin. In St George's Chapel the Duke of Richmond, the Marquess of Hertford and others who had been faithful to the King, entered the building to select a burial site. Inside, the destruction caused during the Civil War was obvious: "... a place which they had been so well acquainted with, they found it so altered and transformed, all inscriptions, and those landmarks pulled down, by which all men knew every particular place in that church, and such a dismal mutation over the whole, they knew not where they were. Nor was there one old officer that had belonged to it, or knew where our princes had used to be interred."

A grave had been dug on the south side of the communion table but the officials decided that Charles should be interred in a vault. Some confusion existed about where a suitable vault could be found, until, searching the choir, "directed by one of the aged poor Knights, did light on a vault in the middle thereof". The vault was cramped and they had to stoop because of the low ceiling, and there were two lead coffins already in place. The larger, with its foot towards the east, was thought to contain the body of Henry VIII, the other, "of moderate proportion", the remains of Jane Seymour. However, there was enough space left for Charles I's coffin.

The King's body was carried to St George's chapel, "being borne by the soldiers of the garrison. Over it a black velvet hearse cloth". Herbert, one of the King's servants who attended the funeral, reported that "the sky was serene and clear, but presently it began to snow, and the snow fell so fast, that by the time the corpse had reached the west end of the chapel, the black pall was all white". Some thought this was a heavenly sign of the King's innocence. The Bishop of London stood weeping, unable to speak: "... there was therefore nothing read at the grave, though the Bishop's lips were observed to move." In the vault "a scarf of lead was provided some two foot long, and five inches broad" on which the Duke of Richmond marked the words KING CHARLES 1648. Then a workman cut the letters out with a chisel and a plumber soldered the lead to the coffin "about the breast of the corpse". An entry to mark the burial was also made in the town's register: "Feb 9. King Charles in the Castle."

The effect on Windsor of the execution of a King may have been dramatic. Those who supported and many who opposed Charles I's reign must have been stunned by the way events turned out. During the Civil War the town had suffered years of depression, and the Commonwealth offered little in the way of prosperity.

John Evelyn made a melancholy visit six years later and entered in his diary: "saw the Castle and Chapel of St George, where they have laid our blessed Martyr, King Charles, in the vault just before the altar. The church and workmanship in stone is admirable. The Castle itself is large in circumference; but the rooms melancholy, and of ancient magnificence ... That night, we lay at Reading. Saw my Lord Craven's house at Caversham, now in ruins, his goodly woods felling by the Rebels."

As the years passed, the location of the vault containing Charles I's coffin was forgotten and eventually controversy arose about its contents. Some even doubted that it contained a body. In 1813, when the vault was re-discovered by workmen, the Prince Regent (later George IV) decided to settle the issue. A master-mason and master-plumber were called in to help Sir Henry Halford, President of the Royal College of Physicians, examine the contents of the coffin. All were sworn to secrecy but within a few days the news leaked out. Features of the long oval face were undoubtedly recognised, though it was "dark and discoloured". The pointed beard was perfect, and the hair thick at the back of the head and nearly black. The head, with a reddish brown beard, was loose and they lifted it up for a closer look. "On holding up the head, the muscles of the neck had evidently contracted considerably, and the fourth cervical vertebra was cut through transversely, leaving the substance of the divided portions smooth and even: an appearance which could only have been produced by a heavy blow from a very sharp instrument, and which furnished the last proof wanting to identify Charles I." At the same time the opportunity was taken to have a look at Henry VIII. "Much like a butcher, only somewhat paler", was the verdict.

A number of castles in England were so badly damaged in the Civil War that they were beyond repair and were abandoned. The usefulness of those which had survived was in doubt and most were dismantled on the orders of Parliament. Windsor Castle nearly suffered the same fate; it escaped by one vote in Parliament. They decided the building was to be retained "for the public use of the Commonwealth". Had the building been demolished and the lands sold, the effect on the town would have been tremendous; and the subsequent development of Windsor a very different story.

64. Oliver Cromwell (with decapitated head of Charles I). From a Dutch engraving.

65. Small brass cannon given by the Armourers Company of London to Charles I as a present for his son.

VII A New Beginning

"The Mayor and Corporation together with divers freemen and inhabitants of the borough aforesaid together with divers of the Militia did in the Town Hall proclaim King Charles the second King of England, Scotland, France and Ireland &c. with all joy acclamations".

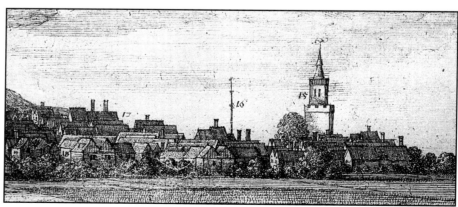

66. Charles II (1660-85).

Though routine life continued during the Commonwealth, the castle lay virtually empty. It was mainly used as a prison, a military barracks, and a refuge for wives and children of Parliamentary soldiers killed or maimed during the wars. In the town people were burdened with higher taxes and the Corporation struggled to raise funds to repair the borough's amenities.

The fortunes of Windsor have always risen or fallen along with the prosperity and popularity of the monarchy. New vigour was assured when, on 12 May 1660 Mr. Galland, an innkeeper and Windsor's Mayor, along with the council dressed in corporation gowns, and with trumpets and drums playing, announced that Charles II was King of England.

Charles II adopted Windsor as his main summer residence. This provided the signal for rejuvenating buildings which had been neglected during the Civil War. There was a new "chimney for the Town Hall" and the much abused Market Cross was renovated. Repairs were carried out to the church and 2s. 6d. paid for "setting up the King's Arms". The mace, which had become "much bruised and squatted" was overhauled and decorated with royal symbols, and silver flagons, cups and plate, previously stored in the Town Hall for safety, were brought out and restored to the churchwardens. The Council decided to re-instate the old custom of feasting and voted £20 be allocated to the Mayor for that purpose.

67. Windsor parish church with maypole to the left which stood in Peascod Street. Drawing by Wenceslaus Hollar c. 1666.

68. Charles II watching racing at Datchet in August 1682.

The poor who inhabited parts of the castle were ejected and a new tennis court built for the amusement of the Royal party. The parks in Windsor Forest were re-stocked with deer, and to satisfy the new monarch's love of the sport, horse-racing was introduced on the Flats at Datchet. Narcissus Luttrel noted in his diary, "The 24th, were several horse-races at Datchet ferry, near Windsor, where his majesty and many of the nobility were present." Money was allocated to pay bell ringers when the King arrived or departed the borough and, as a special treat for the ringers to celebrate his coronation and birthdays, bread and beer was provided. The streets were especially cleaned in preparation for visits and on one occasion Mr. Newman received £2 for gilding the church clock dial. The Corporation had to find sites to accommodate new houses for the influx of wealthy residents attracted by the Court.

Charles II introduced the hearth tax which imposed a levy of two shillings for every fireplace in a house. The returns for 1663 illustrate that Windsor had more than its fair share of large houses. Over a quarter had six or more fire places. Twenty-two of these had ten or more, indicating that their owners were indeed prosperous. Forty-three per cent of the population lived comfortably with three to five fireplaces. The remainder, 71 out of the 271 houses assessed, had one or two hearths. Those considered too poor were not required to pay the tax.

69. Windsor parish church is at the centre with Earl Marshall's (now King Edward III's) Tower on the left and Watch (now Queen's) Tower on the right. Drawing by Wenceslaus Hollar c. 1666.

Merchants and traders earned a living by providing services or goods, rather than in manufacturing, supplying household items, food, clothing and medical needs, and keeping inns. Others worked in the building trades, on the river or in agriculture. Much of the town's prosperity came from trade generated in its markets, fairs and shops, and supplying the needs of the Court.

This rosy picture, however, is counterbalanced by overcrowding and poverty, which was widespread. It is unlikely that the situation for the poor had improved since a petition in 1660 called Windsor "a great and very dear market town of 2000 people, many very poor". Three years after the Restoration, innkeepers complained that soldiers enlisted to serve the castle were still being billeted on them, causing impoverishment. Even the wealthy began to leave. By 1666 the Corporation was obliged to point out to the King that the town had become "much forsaken by the gentry" and that "many of the best householders leave".

70. Windsor in 1666 with St George's Chapel showing above the castle walls. On the extreme left is a maypole and next to it the Bell (now Curfew) Tower. Note the windmill towards the right. Drawing by Wenceslaus Hollar.

At the beginning of Charles II's reign, the interior of St George's Chapel lay virtually in ruins and large sums of money had to be raised to re-furnish it. Money was also needed to provide new service ornaments which had been taken in the Civil War. James, Duke of York (later King James II), donated plate valued at £100. The Earl of Southampton helped solve the problem when he created a Statute allowing the Dean to collect £20 from each newly appointed Knight Companion. There were many vacancies of the Order and King Charles was not slow to elect new Knights. Their £20 levies provided money to help pay for gilt flagons, basins, chalices and candlesticks.

The results were witnessed by Samuel Pepys who attended the Garter Ceremony in 1666. "It is a noble place indeed, and a good choir of voices. Great bowing by all the people, the poor Knights in particular, to the Altar. After prayers, we to see the plate of the chapel, and the robes of Knights, and a man to show us the banners of the several Knights in being, which hung up over the stalls."

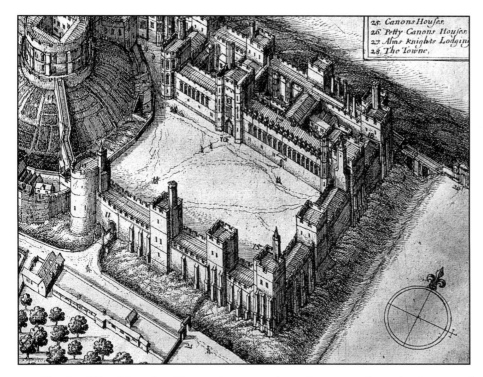

Key within image:
25. Canons Houses.
26. Petty Canons Houses
27. Alms knights Lodging
28. The Towne,

71. Upper Ward of Windsor Castle from a drawing by Hollar made in about 1666. The building still retained its medieval appearance. Note the ditch around the walls and two bridges giving access to the Castle.

Charles II had lived in France for a number of years and no doubt envied the magnificent palaces of Louis XIV, very unlike Windsor Castle which retained its image of a medieval fortress. Large expanses of blank walls had few windows to give light to rooms inside. If the castle was to become a palace worthy of an English King, major restorations would have to be carried out. The English diarist John Evelyn wrote, in August 1670: "Windsor was now going to be repaired, being exceedingly ragged and ruinous."

The architect Hugh May drew up the plans for alterations and many rooms around the quadrangle were entirely rebuilt. These form the suite known today as the State Apartments, and between 1676 and 1681 Antonio Verrio, the Italian painter, decorated the huge ceilings. King Charles also used Verrio to paint the staircases of the house in the town which he had made available for Nell Gwynne, his favourite mistress.

John Evelyn met the artist and became attracted by his work. "After dinner I visited that excellent painter Verrio, whose work in *fresco* in the King's palace, at Windsor, will celebrate his name as long as those walls last. He showed us his pretty garden, choice flowers, and curiosities, he himself being a skilful gardener ... Verrio's invention is admirable." Evelyn showed great insight when he commented on how long Verrio's work would last: "his ordnance full and flowing, antique and heroical; his figures move; and, if the walls hold (which is the only doubt, by reason of the salts which in time and in this moist climate prejudice), the work will preserve his name to ages". Some of the walls and ceilings had to be replaced less than 150 years later.

Three stages in the development of St George's Hall.

72. *As seen by Wenceslaus Hollar in 1663 during a Garter dinner.*

73. *Watercolour c. 1819 showing the frescoes painted by Antonio Verrio. Evelyn's concern that Verrio's work would only last "if the walls will hold" was justified. It became necessary to completely reconstruct the interior of the Hall when work was carried out on the castle under King George IV.*

74. *Painting by Nash showing the Hall during a Garter dinner in Victoria's reign and illustrating how the building changed following its Gothic conversion during George IV's reign. Few changes have been made since.*

Sir Christopher Wren, son of Dr. Christopher Wren, the Dean of Windsor, was appointed Surveyor General. He said of Verrio: "every article of his bill is very modest, and that he highly deserves what he demands".

As time passed, people became more critical of Verrio's work; Tighe and Davis wrote, "Verrio's deficiencies as a painter are neither few nor trifling; but, whatever his merits or demerits may be, his paintings at Windsor Castle, and even some of the rooms which they decorated, are now the subject of history, and some notice of them must not be omitted."

In 1840, Ambrose Poynter, the distinguished architect, found words of praise as well as criticism. "If the suite of apartments, did honour to the eminent architect who superintended their construction and decoration, the same judgment cannot be passed upon the alterations he effected on the exterior of the castle. To open windows in the outer walls, and to give the apartments on all sides the advantage of looking upon the beautiful scenes they command, was a measure both tasteful and judicious, and in the imperishable facing of heath stone which replaced the friable surface of the old building, we recognise the architect who never suffered utility to be a secondary consideration in his works; but while he broke up the gloomy character of the ancient castle, and re-established the durability of its structure, he unfortunately swept away nearly every trace of the architecture of the Middle Ages, so beautiful in itself and so valuable in its associations, and substituted nothing in its place ... as he could not Italianize the whole Castle and would not Gothicize his new building, he seems to have devised the unhappy expedient of obliterating all architectural character whatever."

75. *Sir Christopher Wren, son of the Dean of Windsor.*

Prince Rupert had earned the title of 'Mad Cavalier' from his exploits in the Civil War. He was appointed Constable of the Castle and by 1670 was using accommodation in the Round Tower. Evelyn thought that the Prince had handsomely decorated the keep with "pikes, muskets, pistols, bandoleers, holster, drums, back, breast, and head pieces, as was very extraordinary".

Prince Rupert became interested in scientific research and is credited with inventing an improved gunpowder. In about 1679 he witnessed a trial given by Thomas Charles, engineer of the Mint, of "newly invented guns from pistol to the biggest cannon which with less powder will shoot further than any others".

Charles II held a right of way over private land which stretched from the castle to the Great Park and, when it came up for sale in 1680, the Crown bought it for £1242 4s. 9d. This was the setting for a long avenue of trees which became known as the Long Walk. "The King", wrote Evelyn, "passed most of his time in hunting stag and walking in the park, which he was now planting with rows of trees." Simon Smith of Old Windsor was employed to put new paling round the entire circumference of the Great Park, a task which took six years.

In 1680, a statue of King Charles, dressed as Caesar, was erected at the centre of the Upper Quadrangle. It had been commissioned by Tobias Rustat who employed the Italian artist Josias Stads to create the sculpture and Grinling Gibbons, master carver to the crown, to make the marble pedestal. Evelyn saw the result and found more to say about the sculptor than of his work. "There

76. Charles II's statue shown here in its present position near the Round Tower. It was moved in 1827 when reconstruction work was carried out.

was erected in the court the king on horseback, lately cast in copper, and set on a rich pedestal of White marble, the work of Mr. Gibbons, at the expense of Toby Rustat, a page of the back stairs, who by his wonderful frugality, had arrived to a great estate in money, and did many works of charity as well as this of gratitude to his master, which cost him £1000. He is a very simple, ignorant, but honest and loyal creature."

Horace Walpole thought little of the statue but liked the pedestal: "Gibbons, whose art penetrated all materials, carved that beautiful pedestal in marble for the equestrian statue of the king in the principal court. The fruit, fish, and implements of shipping are all excellent; but the man and the horse may serve as a sign to draw the passenger's eye to the pedestal."

King Charles witnessed a demonstration of a new water supply to the castle in July 1681 — "an extraordinary engine lately invented by Sir Samuel Morland". *The London Gazette* reported that it took "the strength of 4 men" to work it and force "water through a leaden pipe, of an inch and three quarters bore into a vessel placed on the Terrace Walk and gauged exactly for that purpose, at the rate of above sixty barrels an hour". King Charles timed the flow himself with his watch.

Some disbelieved the machine's capabilities and another experiment was organised the following month in front of an equally impressive gathering. "The King, Queen and Prince of Orange [were] attended by divers foreign ambassadors and other persons of eminent quality, and not a few of the English nobility, together with a numerous train of near 1000 persons." They witnessed eight men pump "water (mingled with a vessel of red wine to make it more visible) in a continual stream at the rate of above sixty barrels an hour". Their Majesties were full of admiration and the gathering "unanimously concluded that this was the boldest and most extraordinary experiment that had ever been performed by water in any part of the world".

The pump must have been working efficiently three years later when John Evelyn wrote in his diary: "nor less observable and famous is the throwing so huge a quantity of excellent water to the enormous height of the castle, for the use of the whole house, by an extraordinary invention of Sir Samuel Morland".

Tobacco had been introduced into England in 1565 and when Paul Hentzner made his journey to England in 1598 he noted that smoking was widespread: "... the English are constantly smoking tobacco, and in this manner: they have pipes on purpose made of clay, into the farther end of which they put the Herb, so dry that it may be rubbed into powder, and putting fire to it, they draw the smoke into their mouths, which they puff out again, through their nostrils". The habit spread to Windsor where the mayor and councillors smoked pipes to celebrate special events. In 1671 four shillings were paid out of the Chamberlain's accounts for "tobacco & pipes used at the Town Hall when the King came". Tobacco was thought to be a disinfectant, being particularly effective against the plague, and boys at Eton were compelled to smoke in the school. One boy was actually flogged for not smoking.

Good communications between Windsor and London were essential, particularly when the Court resided in the borough. Ministers and couriers travelled back and forth on matters of state and Charles II became a commuter by making daily visits to Westminster. A coach service was operating in 1673 and *The London Gazette* advertised the service: "... there goes a post constantly from the General Post Office in Bishopsgate Street to Windsor, and another arrives there every morning from thence; and that care will be taken for the safe and speedy conveyance of all Letters which are either delivered in at the General Post Office, or left at the usual places appointed to receive them."

There were of course those who objected, particularly as their livelihood became undermined. "Those coaches hinder the breeding of watermen and much discourage those that are bred; for, there being stage-coaches set up into every little town upon the river Thames, on both sides of the water ... these are they who carry all the letters, little bundles, and passengers, which before they set up, were carried by water, and kept watermen in a full employment."

However, coach services had arrived and other operators, such as John Agars and Partners, Hackney Coachmen, were given a licence in 1687 to ply for trade on Castle Hill, provided they kept "free passage for coaches, wagons and other carriages to and from the upper gate". In 1858, Tighe and Davis observed: "It is probable that the Castle Hill has continued from that day to the present as a stand for vehicles for hire; cabriolets and flies being substituted for hackney coaches, and the general position removed somewhat further from the walls of the Castle." From that day to this, drivers have waited there for customers who require transport from the castle.

77. A mixture of horse and motor transport waits for customers below the Curfew Tower in about 1920. The site is still used as a taxi stand.

Narcissus Luttrel, a prolific recorder of events, wrote in his diary of an exceptionally dry spell of weather in the summer of 1681. In June he wrote, "Windsor Forest is on fire ... this dry weather contributing much to the running and spreading thereof." The following month he reported "a terrible fire in Windsor, which burned down the inns called Garter and White Hart, and several houses". Prince Rupert, who was then over sixty, and a few weeks earlier had been described by Luttrel as "very ill, without hope of recovery", took command and the fire was put out.

The Guildhall was said to be "in a ruinous state" and it was decided that it was "to be pulled down and the materials sold" to make way for a new hall. On 5 September 1687 Windsor's officials paid £1 to entertain "Mr. Clarke's men, masons and bricklayers for a dinner at the first stone setting of the Town Hall". Sir Thomas Fitz (or Fitch), surveyor of the Cinque Ports, designed the building and used workers from the castle to help build it. But he died a few months after the work commenced and Sir Christopher Wren completed it.

The new Guildhall was ready by October 1689 but, if we are to believe the familiarly quoted story, the authorities were not satisfied. "It is said that the municipal authorities after the completion of this building had doubts as to its stability and insisted that Wren should support the span of the first floor with additional pillars. The architect humoured them by building the pillars, but left a space between the tops of them and the roof."

78. The much discussed Guildhall columns with gaps at their tops.

When Celia Fiennes, the daughter of a Cromwellian colonel, visited Windsor in 1698, she described the town as "well built ... something suitable to London by reason of its affinity to the Court ... the streets large, the Market Cross [Guildhall] on stone pillars and a large Hall on the top, from thence the street runs along to the bridge over the Thames and a quarter of a mile off, though indeed there is buildings all along, there is Eton College, a good stone building carved on the outside".

79. The Guildhall completed by Wren and described as having "a spacious large room, well adapted for the meeting of the mayor and corporation for business of the borough."

VIII Change of Faith

"I have received an account of the Queen's pregnancy which gives me good cause to suspect that there is some trickery afoot".

80. James II (1685-88).

James Stewart, Charles II's brother, had secretly married Anne Hyde, a girl said to be far below his social position, in November 1659. The following year they re-married at a public ceremony, a few weeks before their first child was born. Eleven years later Anne died after giving birth to her eighth child. Only two, Mary and Anne, lived beyond childhood and are of concern to Windsor.

In 1673 James married an Italian Princess, Mary Beatrice of Modena, who was 25 years his junior. They had a number of children, but none were alive in February 1685 when James Stewart was proclaimed King. *The London Gazette* recorded that in Windsor "the great guns were thrice discharged and the day ended with bonfires and other expressions of joy".

James was a committed Catholic and set on a course of uniting England under that faith. He employed Verrio to decorate the chapel which Cardinal Wolsey had planned for his own tomb, and fitted it out with ornaments for Catholic worship. But his actions were not popular in the town: "to the great disgust of his protestant subjects, [the King] publicly attended therein a celebration of mass".

In order to strengthen relations with Rome, James II received Monsignor Ferdinand D'Adda, the Pope's diplomatic representative at Windsor in July 1687. It was an event which, if not popular with the protestant population, filled the town to capacity: "... some of the inhabitants were astonished; and it was very difficult to get provisions or room either for horse or man". It was the first visit by a Pope's minister for more than 140 years and the large crowd had a long wait for his arrival. The emissary was due at noon, but did not appear till early evening. The procession filled the streets, "36 coaches, 6 horses each", with the Pope's envoy "clothed in purple, and a gold crucifix hanging at his breast", accompanied by the Duke of Grafton and Sir George Cotterel.

James II's attempt to convert England may have been tolerated by the population who were secure in the knowledge that Princess Mary, a devout Protestant, was the heiress presumptive. She had married William, Prince of Orange, who shared her ambitions to inherit the British throne and, after all, the King was over fifty.

When it was announced that Queen Mary was pregnant, the Protestants were alarmed by the thought that she might bear a son. Some believed the priests were even prepared to swap the baby for a boy if the necessity arose. Princess Mary also feared there might be subterfuge. "I have received an

81. Princess Mary Beatrice of Modena who became the second wife of James II.

54

account of the Queen's pregnancy which gives me good cause to suspect that there is some trickery afoot", she wrote in April 1688. In June the Queen gave birth to a boy in St James's Palace and the Catholic courtiers were delighted that the line of succession had now changed.

Rumours continued to spread in an attempt to discredit the birth: "... tis said the queen was very quick, so that few persons were by", wrote Narcissus Luttrel. Mrs. Wilkins, the midwife, was paid 500 guineas for her part in the birth and the Queen's physician received a knighthood. Some said the Queen had not even been pregnant and believed the baby had been put into a warming pan and smuggled into her bed.

In Windsor, the Corporation were obliged to dress in their gowns and go in procession to the market where a bonfire was lit, and beer and claret was provided for the people to celebrate the safe delivery of the Prince.

The Royal family arrived in the borough the following month but did not stay long. The Prince was a weak, sickly baby, and his health grew worse. The party moved to Richmond where he made a recovery, but only after Mrs. Cooper, a tiler's wife, was employed wearing "cloth petticoat and waistcoat, and old shoes and no stockings", to suckle the baby. The Royal family returned to Windsor in early August as unrest concerning a Catholic revival continued. The Dutch navy was encouraged to put to sea by news of a mass of support awaiting them in England and the "Protestant Wind" carried the ships to Brixham where, on 5 November 1688, William of Orange landed in a bid to uphold his and Mary's claim.

Many sympathisers joined the Prince as his troops made their way through Exeter, Oxford and Wallingford. There was even time for the Prince to admire the Earl of Pembroke's collection of Van Dycks at Wilton. In Reading a slight skirmish occurred when the Prince's advance guard met King James's forces and some troops were killed. The Dutch and their English supporters won the battle and gained the town. Within days the Prince was in Windsor where he convened a council of leading peers. Retiring to bed he left them to discuss what to do. They agreed that King James must relinquish the Crown, but by then he was already humiliated and planning to flee to the safety of France.

82. River Thames with Windsor Bridge on right and Curfew Tower in the background. From a painting by S. Owen.

83. Queen Anne (1702-14).

People in Windsor were no doubt pleased by the events, though most of the Council appointed by James II lost their jobs. New councillors were duly appointed to administer the town from the new Guildhall, and over £20 was spent on a ceremony to acclaim William III and Mary II as joint rulers (1689-1702. Queen Mary died in 1694).

Despite Windsor's enthusiastic reception, William and Mary spent most of their time at Hampton Court, only visiting Windsor occasionally. But Princess Anne, James II's second daughter, became very fond of Windsor and she, with her husband Prince George of Denmark, used Nell Gwynne's house as a summer residence. They had 17 children but sadly only five were born alive, and the longest survivor, the Duke of Gloucester, died at Windsor in 1700, on his 11th birthday.

Queen Anne acceded on the death of William III and, despite being over-weight, prematurely aged and crippled with gout, she was kindly, warm-hearted and loved by the crowds at Windsor. She was fond of horses and constructed a carriage road in the Great Park, which Jonathan Swift, the English satirist, described in a letter as "the finest riding upon artificial roads, made on purpose for the queen". Queen Anne rode and hunted in a single-seated chaise, with extra large wheels: "... she hunts in a chaise with one horse, which she drives herself, and drives furiously like Jehu, and is a mighty hunter, like Nimrod". The following month, Swift wrote: "the queen was hunting the stag till four this afternoon, and she drove in her chaise forty miles, and it was five before we went to dinner". Queen Anne enjoyed horse-racing, too, and did much to popularise the sport. Jointly with the town she donated prizes for the winners. "Yesterday was a great horse race at Datchet", Luttrel wrote in 1709, "Colonel Moreton won the Queen's Plate, and the Earl of Bridgewater that of the Town of Windsor." Two years later Jonathan Swift took a ride on open heath to the south-west of the Great Park and saw the preparations for a new race-course at Ascot: "we saw a place they have made for a famous horse-race tomorrow, where the Queen will come".

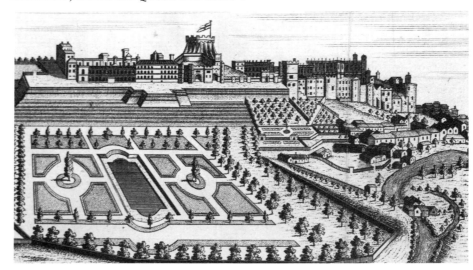

84. Plan view of the garden in the Little Park, begun during Queen Anne's reign but later abandoned.

Queen Anne often supported enterprises undertaken by the borough. The majority of children received little or no education and when the Mayor and Corporation, the Vicar and the Dean and Canons of St George's Chapel launched an appeal to raise funds for a Free School, she subscribed £50 annually to help provide free education to 70 children of poor families. The plan took a number of years to take shape and was substantially helped by the will of Theodore Randue, a citizen of Windsor. In 1724 he bequeathed £550 to the project which enabled the school to open two years later.

In the meantime, the town decided to pay a tribute to the Queen by placing a statue of her on the Guildhall. Mr. Penington received 6s. 3d. for doing the work. In 1713, a statue of Prince George of Denmark, presented by Christopher Wren, son of the architect, was erected at the Guildhall's opposite end.

The main route from London to Windsor Castle passed down Eton High Street, over the toll bridge which crossed the Thames, and on to the castle. An alternative route went via Datchet Ferry. This had been used by travellers since at least 1278, when the keeper, appropriately called John le Passur, was given a "great oak" for building a boat at Datchet.

85. Queen Anne's bridge crossing the Thames at Datchet c. 1780.

In 1706, Queen Anne decided to replace the ferry with a bridge, "for making a more commodious way for Her Majesty with her coaches". This made access from Datchet much easier but it was not popular in Windsor. John Andrews, who had leased the right to collect tolls on Windsor's bridge, found it particularly unsatisfactory. He complained to the borough who in turn protested to the Lord High Treasurer. "Your petitioners ... humbly beg leave to represent to your Lordships that the ancient tolls of Windsor bridge are much lessened by erecting of the New Bridge whereby both the corporation and their tenants are great sufferers."

86. Windsor toll bridge which lost trade when the bridge at Datchet was built. From a water colour attributed to Paul Sandby, c. 1760.

Mr. Travers, the Queen's Surveyor General replied saying: "though I think the corporation can have no demand in Law, for satisfaction of this loss ... I do not think it unreasonable for her Majesty to give the corporation £55 and their undertenant John Andrews £25 in full satisfaction for all the aforesaid damage." These terms appear to have satisfied the Mayor and bailiffs.

Queen Anne's successors, George I and II, did not find Windsor to their taste. For nearly sixty years the castle was virtually abandoned as a royal residence. Inevitably, the town and castle suffered. Lack of interest resulted in the Duke of Norfolk, Constable of the Castle and High Steward of the Borough, allowing Elizabeth Edwards to run business premises inside the walls. She was a seamstress with many children to support, whose husband had fallen into debt, and she was about to lose her home. To prevent her becoming a burden on the parish, the Duke issued a warrant allowing her to "place a shop not exceeding twenty foot in length, and three foot in breadth" within the gate of the lower ward of the castle.

This was only one example of encroachment on the castle during a period of neglect. More houses sprang up beside the walls in Thames Street and an assortment of workers and others secured lodgings within the walls. The best furnishings and pictures were moved to London, cleaning and maintenance were neglected, and the whole structure fell into a state of decay.

By 1730, the Round Tower needed repairing, particularly the roof which had become "in danger of falling", and the stairs were described as "in so ruinous a condition that they are almost now and will soon be entirely useless". Any work undertaken was to be "in the best but cheapest manner", with a maximum budget of £200.

Supervision over Windsor Forest also lapsed. For centuries it had provided an ideal habitat for rogues and highwaymen. Maidenhead Thicket, where the main road to the west passed through the forest, became particularly notorious as a resort for highwaymen. Luttrel wrote of six highwaymen who robbed nearly fifty people in January 1695, and of a man who was shot dead and robbed of 100 guineas four years later. In 1700, there was more shooting when a number of men held up the coach on its way to Bath. The local parson received extra pay because he had to ride regularly through the area.

The road from Windsor to London was no better. In 1683, it was reported that seven robberies had been committed in recent weeks and a warrant was sent to Sir Francis Compton, Major of the Earl of Oxford's Regiment of Horse, to patrol the highway every day until further notice and apprehend all highwaymen and robbers. Capital punishment did nothing to deter the men. There were regular hangings at Tyburn, often of four or five people at a time. On 12 December 1694, eighteen were executed in one day, eight of them for being highwaymen.

Four members of one gang which had committed a number of robberies in the area were pursued to Old Windsor and arrested in 1698. Even though poaching with a gun carried the death penalty, it was widespread. One gang known as 'The Blacks', from the practice of blackening their faces like today's commandos, operated over a wide area. For several years they seem to have been impossible to convict until the authorities set a trap to catch the ringleaders. Three of their number were persuaded to give evidence against a clergyman about to be tried for high treason and on the way to court they were arrested. Rewards were offered for the rest of the gang and many were caught. Eventually 40 men appeared at Reading Assizes; four were hanged and most of the others were transported.

87. Datchet Lane. From a painting by Paul Sandy.

Only a few travellers arriving at Windsor in the 18th century left records of their journey. John Macky spent Christmas in the town in 1712 and wrote a letter to "his friend abroad", which provides an insight into Christmas celebrations: "... this being the worst season of the year for travelling and Carnival time: which, contrary to the customs of other countries, where the People, at this season, flock to great towns to participate of the diversions of their several carnivals; here in England, during the Twelve Days of Christmas, the nobility and gentry retire to their respective seat in the country; and there with their relations, neighbours, and tenants, keep carnivals in their own houses, hospitality, music, balls, and play as much during this season all over England, as in any Kingdom whatsoever. And I chose to retire hither, during the deadness of the town, to have the pleasure of giving you the description of the celebrated place with the adjacent Country". John Macky gave a long description of the castle, but had few words to say about the borough. "The town which sends Members to Parliament, but otherwise very inconsiderable, lies on the West side; and its Park, whose walls are washed by the River Thames to the North and East; and a Forest of a vast Extent to the South."

Despite years of neglect of the castle's fabric, Daniel Defoe was able to write in 1724: "the most beautiful, and most pleasantly situated castle, and Royal Palace, in the whole of Britain." Defoe witnessed changes which had occurred as one reign gave way to the next. "In the royal lodgings, there have been so many alterations of furniture, that there can be no entering upon the particular description. In one of those lodgings, the late Queen Mary set up a rich atlas, and chintz bed, which, in those times, was invaluable, the chintz being of Masslapatan, on the coast of Coromandel, the finest that was ever seen before that time in England; but the rate of those things suffered much alterations since that time. Also here was, some time before that, the picture of the late Duchess of Portsmouth [one of Charles II's mistresses] at full length, a noble piece, and of which it was said, King Charles II would say, 'it was the finest painting, of the finest woman in Christendom'; but our English ladies of Queen Mary's court, were of another opinion".

88. The Duchess of Portsmouth.

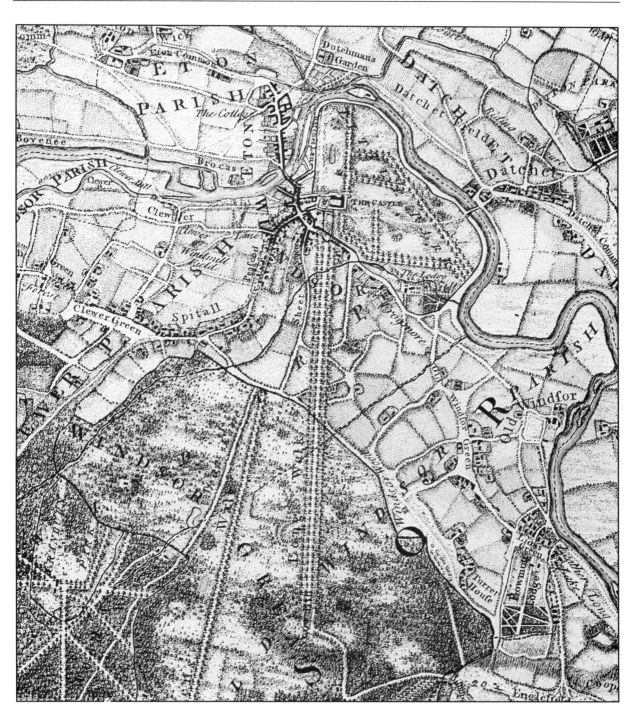

89. John Rocque's survey of Berkshire, dated 1761, showing Queen Anne's bridge at Datchet, and the road to Old Windsor crossing the Long Walk before passing through Frogmore.

90. Sheet Street. From a water colour dated 1775 by Paul Sandy.

91. Windsor Castle and town in 1805.

IX   Joy and Sadness

"... a brutal amusement, which has too frequently occurred at this place, which I would gladly suppress were I possessed of sufficient authority".

During King George III's reign, the bonds between town and castle became firmer than in any previous reign since Henry I first held court there. Even though he purchased Buckingham House, which became better known as Buckingham Palace, where most of his children were born, and for a number of years he rejected the idea of living in the Castle, he became exceptionally fond of Windsor. The town responded by treating him as one of its favourite sovereigns.

The truth is that in Windsor George III adopted the lifestyle of an English gentleman, living quietly with Queen Charlotte and their many children in newly built Queen's Lodge. "Windsor has lately received an additional beauty", declared a guide book, "... on the entrance into the Little Park, named Queen's Lodge ... In front is a beautiful verdure, inclosed by a range of iron palings."

92. George III (1760-1820).

93. Queen's Lodge. Built by George III and demolished by his son George IV as part of his plan to improve the Long Walk.

When George III succeeded his grandfather to the throne in October 1760, the country was experiencing a period of prosperity, and renewed royal interest in Windsor stimulated much needed improvements. The King set an example to other wealthy gentlemen by contributing £1,000 for repairing the streets with heath stone. The roads were in a dreadful condition and an Act "for better paving, cleansing, lighting and watching" was passed in 1769. At night they were particularly unsatisfactory: "... many disorders and irregularities are

94. Henry VIII's Gate,
c. 1780.

frequently committed in the night-time in the said streets and lanes, for want of being properly lighted and watched". The Act recommended that a "competent number of fit and able-bodied men, not exceeding six, to watch and guard the said streets and lanes" be appointed.

Part of the problem came from the fact that Windsor was a garrison town and lacked proper accommodation for the troops. In April 1780, *The Gentleman's Magazine* reported that "a great riot happened at Windsor, between a regiment of militia [Lancashire Volunteers] quartered there and the townsmen, which was terminated by the interposition of a party of horse". The problems were partially eased when better facilities became available for the troops. In 1784 a hospital with two wards to accommodate 20 men each was built on land provided by the Corporation called Glaziers Corner, on the east of the Long Walk. Barracks to accommodate 750 Foot were built in Sheet Street in 1795, and a building to house 400 Cavalry was constructed six years later.

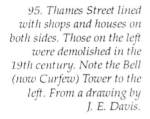

95. Thames Street lined with shops and houses on both sides. Those on the left were demolished in the 19th century. Note the Bell (now Curfew) Tower to the left. From a drawing by J. E. Davis.

Large numbers of troops were attracted by bull baiting, a form of entertainment which continued in Windsor till well into the 19th century. The spectacle appalled Charles Knight (Senior) who was the Mayor in 1818. He called it a "brutal amusement, which has too frequently occurred at this place, which I would gladly suppress were I possessed of sufficient authority".

Pedestrians using Thames Street in George III's Windsor were said to be in "great danger and inconvenience". This was caused by men and horses loading or hauling boats and barges on the river. To remedy this, offenders were obliged to forfeit one horse "with all gear, halters and accoutrements", and pay a 40-shillings fine. Charles Knight (Junior) described Thames Street as narrow and crowded with houses of the meanest character, mostly occupied by disreputable people.

Charles P. Moritz, a "literary gentleman of Berlin", also found reason for complaint against some local people. He was on a walking tour of England and in June 1782 when, dirty, tired and hungry, he sought lunch and a room at Eton's *Christopher Inn*: "... the waiter soon gave me to understand, that I should find no very friendly reception. Whatever I got they seemed to give me with such an air, as showed too plainly how little they thought of me; and as if they considered me but as a beggar ... they told me, that they had no intention of lodging me, as they had no room for such guests."

Moritz decided to try his luck in Windsor and after seeing the sights he entered an inn opposite the castle: "... a very capital inn, where I saw many officers and several persons of consequence going in and out. And here at this inn, contrary to all expectation, I was received by the landlord with a great civility, and even kindness". But the staff was not so pleasant. "The maid, by the order of her master, showed me a room where I might adjust my dress a little; but I could hear her mutter and grumble as she went along with me."

In the evening, Moritz' spirits were revived by a swim in the river and a moonlight walk. "On my return the waiters (who from my appearance, probably expected but a trifling reward for their attentions to me) received me gruffly, and as if they were sorry to see me again. This was not all; I had the additional mortification to be again roughly accosted by the cross maid, who had before shown me to the bed-chamber; and, while dropping a kind of half curtsey, with a suppressed laugh, sneeringly told me, I might look out for another lodging, as I could not sleep there, since the room she had by mistake shown me, was already engaged. It can hardly be necessary to tell you, that I loudly protested against this sudden change. At length the landlord came, and I appealed to him; and he with great courtesy immediately desired another room to be shown me; in which, however, there were two beds; so that I was obliged to admit a companion ..."

"Directly under my room was the tap-room; from which I could plainly hear too much of the conversation of some low people, who were drinking and singing songs, in which, as far as I could understand them, there were many passages at least as vulgar and nonsensical as ours." Charles Moritz left next morning, refused to tip the ill-tempered maid, and continued his walking holiday, cheered on by sunny weather.

In Eton, George III took a fatherly interest in the college and showed more concern for its welfare than many of his predecessors. He often chatted to boys who visited the terrace and on one occasion, after a concert in the castle for the school, invited the boys to supper and sent the masters home hungry. Naturally the boys gave the King rousing receptions when he visited the college.

Charles Moritz had noted the respect in which people held the King. "I did not see a single person, high or low, who did not pull off their hats as their sovereign passed them." George III became such a familiar sight in the streets that townspeople called him "the Squire of Windsor".

Fanny Burney, a famous novelist who was appointed Second Keeper of the robes to Queen Charlotte, wrote: "He knew something of the character and affairs of most persons who live under the shadow of the Castle". He visited local shops with Queen Charlotte and, when elections were being held, canvassed for his favourite candidates. "All the Royal bakers, brewers and butchers had voted against Keppel", wrote Horace Walpole following the election when Admiral Keppel lost his seat.

96. Printing Office and Library, Castle Hill, in 1830 when owned by J. B. Brown.

One businessman who did reject the King's recommendation and voted for Keppel was Charles Knight (Senior). He took an active interest in the parish and Corporation, and was distressed by the treatment of the poor. Knight ran a printing and bookshop at No. 2 Castle Street (later Castle Hill) which George III visited to see the latest publications. Knight's son later wrote of the King: "He had an extraordinary faculty for recognising everybody, young or old".

In his Windsor guide books Knight wrote how George III encouraged local trade: "... their majesties have resided so much here, who, by their benevolent diffusion of their favours, have excited a spirit of industry and emulation in the different tradesmen, who vie with each other in the improvement of their shops and the quality and cheapness of their various commodities, so that most of the necessaries, with many of the superfluities of life, may be purchased here on as suitable terms as at the first shops in the metropolis."

George III's love of the country found an outlet in the improvements he made to parks and local amenities. Queen Anne's bridge at Datchet became impassable, part of it collapsed, and much of the rest was dismantled. George III re-introduced the ferry service and gave the public free passage while discussions took place over a new bridge.

The Crown argued that Berkshire and Buckinghamshire, which administered the river banks, were responsible but they could not agree on a design. Both realised that the existing piles were inadequate to take the weight of stone and Berkshire preferred an iron bridge, while Buckinghamshire favoured one of wood. When the bridge was eventually built, each county took responsibility for its own half. Some iron was used on one side, wood only on the other, and the "junction was clumsily effected ... and the abrupt termination of each party's labours was distinctly visible". Despite the problems, it was opened by Queen Charlotte and Princess Elizabeth in December 1811, amid "great rejoicing".

97. Datchet Bridge c. 1846. It was much argued about and a poor structure when compared with the earlier bridge. From a drawing by J. E. Davis.

Windsor, however, was not associated with spectacle and pageantry at this time. Little use was made of the castle's accommodation and years of neglect had taken their toll. In 1766 Mrs. Philip Lybbe Powys wrote: "I think there is but little worthy of one's observation; the furniture is old and dirty, most of the best pictures removed to the Queen's Palace [Buckingham House] and the whole kept so un-neat, that it hurts one to see almost the only place in England worthy to be styled a King's Palace so totally neglected".

98. *The River Thames at Windsor c. 1823. Painted by W. Wolnoth.*

Charles Knight (Junior) wrote of his "boyish perambulations about Windsor Castle" at the turn of the century. "I come up the paltry wooden stairs that lead from the north terrace, I look into the Quadrangle, which is solitary and silent, except where a stonemason or two are at work ... Adjoining the Deanery is a ruinous building called Wolsey's Tomb-house. St George's Chapel has been restored and beautified; but this building has been neglected since the day of James the Second."

George III was an accomplished artist, a talented draughtsman, and could dismantle and reassemble the most complicated watch mechanism. He was fascinated by scientific instruments and made a friend of William Herschel, a musician who became an eminent astronomer. In 1781 Herschel, who was then living in Bath, discovered the planet Uranus. Later he moved to Slough and King George paid £4,000 for a giant telescope to be erected at the astronomer's home. "The framework of Herschel's telescope formed a conspicuous object for many years", wrote Tighe and Davis in 1858, "as travellers on the coach road between London and Oxford, by way of Henley-on-Thames, may remember. Traces of that memorial of the astronomer still exist, and there is a tablet to his memory in the neighbouring church of Upton."

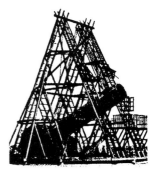

99. *Herschel's telescope, in 1775.*

George III invited Professor Argand of Geneva to come to Windsor in 1783 and demonstrate the mystery of flight with a gas-filled balloon. The professor filled a 30-inch diameter bladder with hydrogen, attached a string to its neck, and handed it to the King. Queen Charlotte and the children watched with amazement from an upper window as the King allowed the balloon to float up and down before cutting the string and letting it fly away.

*100. The South Terrace
with George III and
children c. 1781.
Queen's Lodge is in
the background.*

Scenes on the castle's terraces, where royalty blended happily both with townspeople and visitors, are described in touching detail by Fanny Burney in her diary: "... the princesses and their ladies, and the younger princess, making a very gay and pleasing procession ... Every way they moved, the crowd retired to stand up against the wall as they passed, and then closed in to follow".

Frederick, Duke of York, arrived in 1787 and joined the assembly. "It was indeed an affecting sight to view the general content", wrote Miss Burney, "but that of the king went to my very heart, so delighted he looked — so proud of his son — so benevolently pleased that every one should witness his satisfaction. The terrace was very full; all Windsor and its neighbourhood poured in upon it, to see the prince, whose whole demeanour seemed promising to merit his flattering reception; gay, yet grateful; modest, yet unembarrassed."

Behind this happy picture presented to the world, there was a dark cloud hanging over the Royal family. George III was suffering from a severe mental disorder, and Fanny Burney was able to witness its effect on the King and his family at first hand. "I dreadfully fear he is on the eve of some severe fever", she wrote for 3 November 1788. "The Queen is almost overpowered with some secret terror. I am affected beyond all expression in her presence, to see what struggles she makes to support serenity. To-day she gave up the conflict when I was alone with her, and burst into a violent fit of tears. It was very terrible to see!" The following day passed "much the same as the days preceding it; the Queen in deep distress, the King in a state almost incomprehensible, and all the house uneasy and alarmed."

During the evening of the next day the King's illness appeared worse. "Oh, my dear friends, what history! The King, at dinner, had broken forth into positive delirium, which long had been menacing all who saw him most closely; and the Queen was so overpowered as to fall into violent hysterics. All the Princesses were in misery, and the Prince of Wales had burst into tears. No one knew what was to follow — no one could conjecture the event."

Towards the end of the month, it was decided the King should be moved from the public gaze at Windsor to the privacy of Kew. "The Queen's knowledge of the King's aversion to Kew made her consent to this measure with the extremist reluctance; yet it was not to be opposed: it was stated as much the best for him, on account of the garden: as here there is none but what is public to spectators from the terrace, or tops of houses. I believe they were perfectly right, though the removal was so tremendous."

The King was in tears when a number of local people saw his carriage cross the park for Datchet Bridge. He bowed to them and said to his companion, Colonel Greville: "These good people are too fond of me ... Why am I taken from the place I like best in all the world?"

By March, to the amazement of his doctors, George III recovered sufficiently to return to Windsor. Fanny Burney was defiantly pleased. "All illness over, all fears removed, all sorrows heightened! The King was so well as to go on horseback, attended by a large party of gentlemen ... everything and everybody were smiling and lively. All Windsor came out to meet the King. It was a joy amounting to ecstasy; I could not keep my eyes dry all day long." Fanny Burney's joy was reflected in the people of Windsor who celebrated the event with a display of fireworks.

Once again crowds gathered on the terrace to catch a glimpse of the King. In 1791 Baron J. F. W. van Spaen van Biljoen, while on a tour of English gardens, decided to join them. "Although it was not a Sunday, we came across His Majesty, almost face to face before recognising him, as the King is not followed by a large retinue and nobody bows to him, the only politeness shown being that of standing aside."

George III showed renewed interest in the town and running the parks. He appointed Nathaniel Kent to enclose over a thousand acres of wild uncultivated land in the Great Park and make it suitable for farming. Kent had spent a number of years abroad and was deeply impressed by the agricultural methods practised by the Flemish people. He retired from government service to become a land agent and duly arrived at Windsor in March 1791 to consult with the King and plan the project. Two farms were created. One was run on Flemish lines and the other on the Norfolk principle of crop rotation. Because of his great interest George III soon became known as "Farmer George", a nickname he is said to have relished.

He was also a keen supporter of the theatre company which used a small barn for its performances. In 1793, it moved to an "elegant and commodious Theatre" in the High Street. Boxes, equipped with "capacious armchairs", were reserved for the Royal family and their playbills were printed on silk. But the building was small and, despite George III's patronage, the company had to struggle for survival. The management had a continual battle with Eton College which restricted theatrical entertainments within ten miles of the school, and opposition also came from religious groups. When the theatre's lease expired in 1813, the players moved out and the building was turned into a chapel. When it opened for services, crowds swarmed in and people blocked the doors. The *Express* reported that the building had attracted bigger crowds than when in use as a theatre. The theatre company persevered, however, and two years later a building to accommodate an audience of about five hundred was erected in Thames Street. This burnt down in 1908 and the present building took its place shortly afterwards.

101. Theatre Royal in about 1805 before it burnt down. Today's theatre has an excellent reputation and is well patronised by local residents and visitors. Her Majesty the Queen and other members of the Royal Family also attend performances, continuing the tradition of George III.

102. Eton greets George III as his party returns along the High Street from a hunting expedition. From a painting by Rowlandson.

In the meantime, George III finally decided to take up residence in the castle. Substantial improvements were made under the supervision of James Wyatt which included the renovation of Wolsey's chapel at the east end of St George's. This had become derelict since its use by James II, and George III decided that it should undergo a thorough repair and become a place of interment for his family. His large family dispersed themselves along the castle's numerous corridors to find accommodation in different wings and towers around the quadrangle, and the King occupied a suite overlooking the North Terrace.

On 25 October 1809, when 50 years of the King's reign were celebrated in Windsor's streets, George III, having by then lost his sight, was unable to join the festivities. "The morning was ushered in by the discharge of cannon, ringing of bells etc.", Cornelia Knight wrote when she described the events in her journal. "Afterwards to Mrs. Duval's to see the 'feu de joie', and the troops march past — horse artillery, Blues, Stafford, Windsor, and Clewer volunteers. An ox was roasted whole, and two sheep, in a place called Bachelor's Acre. The Queen, the Princesses, and the Royal Dukes went to see it, and tasted the beef and pudding." Charles Knight (Junior) wrote that he dressed in a "costume of blue coat, white waistcoat, knee-breeches, and silk stockings, to present slices of the ox on a silver salver to the Queen and Princesses". In the evening Cornelia Knight accompanied the Royal party to Frogmore for supper and to see the fireworks. One thousand three hundred tickets had been sent to guests: "The Queen's party was about ninety, consisting, for the most part, of ladies and gentlemen of the neighbourhood who visit their Majesties at the Castle ... Things were not well managed in the gardens, but supper and all the arrangements in the house were very pleasant ... The town was very orderly, though full of people. There were two illuminated arches and several transparencies". Next day celebrations continued: "A bull was baited this morning, and a ball this evening at the Town Hall".

In 1810, John Evans, a baptist minister, spent a week's summer holiday in Windsor with his family. "We entered Windsor about six o'clock, and having refreshed ourselves at the inn with a cup of tea, hastened to the Terrace ... It was seven o'clock, and the good King soon made his appearance with his accustomed punctuality. A little door in the castle was thrown open, when two attendants were seen leading this venerable personage with great care down a flight of steps till he safely alighted upon the terrace. The Princesses Elizabeth and Augusta accompanied him, one on each side, or rather took hold of his arm; they paced backwards and forwards for an hour ... His want of sight is very apparent, for his hat is drawn over the upper part of this face, and he feels about with his cane."

The death of the King's youngest daughter, Princess Amelia, in 1810 brought on another attack of insanity. By the following February the King's health had deteriorated severely, and the Prince of Wales took on the role of Regent.

It is unlikely that George III was able to appreciate the country's success at Waterloo in 1815 which brought an end to the Napoleonic Wars. The Duke of Wellington had already been given a good reception in Windsor the previous year when he came to review his regiment. As he entered the town, he was met by a large number of townspeople who removed the horses from his carriage and themselves hauled it the rest of the way to the *Castle Inn*. Later in the day the Corporation assembled in the Guildhall and resolved to present the Duke with the Honorary Freedom of the Corporation and a gold box.

A courier was sent from London to Windsor with the news of Wellington's victory and, as he passed through Eton, the boys threw their hats in the air. Many boys were at the barrack gates to welcome the Guards and Blues as they returned, and were in the Long Walk when a dinner was given to the soldiers. Tables were laid out under the trees in long rows and all Windsor and the surrounding gentry were present. "It was a splendid day, and a glorious sight — enough to make the heart warm, considering that every one of the guests had been through the fiercest baptism of fire of the age."

George III spent his last years in Windsor Castle, progressively going blind, deaf and insane. He died on 29 January 1820.

103. King George III at Windsor in old age.

X No Expense Spared

"... do everything in a substantial manner, and not merely vamp the building".

The living standards of many townspeople improved during George III's reign but, as Charles Knight (Junior) wrote, in the 19th century there were large numbers of impoverished people in Windsor. "The misery of the poor in my native town at the beginning of the century was sufficiently visible even to my childish apprehension." The poor demonstrated against the price of bread, as Knight recalled: "... a furious mob gathering at the junction of the streets near the market-place ... They had smashed windows of several bakers in the lower part of the town. They believed, as the greater number of people everywhere believed, that the high price of corn was wholly occasioned by combinations of corn-factors, meal-men, millers, and bakers". The mob attacked the baker's shop next door to the Knight home. "He cared little if his door were forced, and his loaves stolen, provided the heavy box under his bed were safe. That box, as he more than once showed me, was full of crowns and half crowns, with some bright guineas, which he had long hoarded ... My father from his window exhorted the people to go home. I stood trembling behind him, and was somewhat astonished to see how powerful was the influence of firmness and kindness in turning aside the wild but unpremeditated excitement of unhappy and ignorant men, who were not without a sense of justice even in their anger."

To ease the situation, a canteen was opened in a house "which had been fitted up with coppers, wherein unlimited shins of beef became reduced into savory soup, and bushels of rice were boiled into a palatable mess".

"Never was there such a sink of impurity as my native town", Knight recalled. "... In Bachelor's Acre the 'little victims' played by the side of a great open cesspool, kept brimming and overflowing by drains disgorging from every street. The Court sniffed this filthy reek. In the fields around Frogmore it tainted the cowslip and the hawthorn blossom. Municipal or royal dignitaries never interfered to abate or remove the nuisance."

Young children could earn a few coppers by becoming chimney sweeps. They climbed the inside of chimneys of large houses to brush them down, and were easily recognised by their soot-covered bodies and tattered clothing. Some, according to the *Express*, "go about almost naked and in a filthy condition on the Sabbath". This led the Mayor to hold a meeting in an attempt to have the "urchins" washed and properly clothed on Sundays, but it was pointed out that the little money they earned was not sufficient to buy clothing.

104. Chimney sweep and his young assistant. From Cries of London.

Some children went into service at an early age. Karina Skinner, a girl of about 13, was a servant to Mr. Trigge of Eton. In January 1814 Mr. Trigge's pump stopped working and Karina took a kettle to get water from the Thames. Unfortunately the poor girl slipped and was drowned. That winter was particularly cold; in late January the Thames froze over and an ice carnival was held on the river near Windsor Bridge.

Little by little the situation for the poor improved as dedicated people gave a lead. Edward Hawke Locker, who was born in Kent, educated at Eton, and became Secretary to Admiral Sir Edward Pellew, settled in Windsor in later life. He was appalled by the complete lack of medical facilities for ordinary people and in 1817 put forward a scheme to establish a free dispensary. Queen Charlotte and her daughters gave their patronage and, at a public meeting in the Guildhall, the plan was approved. When the dispensary opened in 1818, Dr. Stewart became the Consulting Physician, John O'Reilly, John Chapman and William Rendall, Surgeon-Apothecaries, and William Jones its resident House-Dispenser. William Jones proved to be very unpopular and was replaced within a few months, after being reprimanded by the Committee and told to use milder language with his patients. Edward Locker was also a main driving force in creating the National School which catered for two hundred boys and two hundred girls on Maids' Acres.

In a "great ceremony and Masonic splendour", the foundation stone of a cast-iron bridge between Windsor and Eton was laid in July 1822. Its completion was delayed when Mr. William Moore, the contractor, died on the site, leaving his son John to finish the work. Another delay occurred when draining the site for the foundation for one of the piers. This was overcome by using four chain pumps and a steam engine, working day and night, to drain the area. The bridge finally opened on 1 June 1824. Afterwards the assembled dignitaries filed into the *Swan Inn* for a banquet.

105. Windsor Bridge, 1850, designed by Charles Hollis. An Act of Parliament allowed tolls to be collected to defray costs. From a drawing by J. Carter dated 1850.

106. Windsor parish church from Norden's map of 1607. Even then the tower required a buttress for support.

Underestimating building costs and rising prices are not new phenomena, as repairs to the castle and church in the early 19th century demonstrate. In 1793, Charles Knight (Senior) described the parish church as "a spacious ancient ill-built fabric, the pews being so constructed and appropriated, as to exclude a majority of the inhabitants for attending Divine Service". The structure was also dilapidated and unsafe, the belfry and tower being particularly weak. Repairs were carried out but time proved them to be only of temporary use. The old building could not be saved, and in 1820 work began on a new church. It opened for services in 1822.

The original costs were estimated at £9,000, but this proved to be inadequate. The eventual bill came to £14,000 and left a debt that took 17 years to clear. King George IV helped by donating over £1,000.

The relationship between George IV and Windsor was not as intimate as that experienced during his father's reign. The borough saw little of him before or after the official reception on 1 October 1823, when he arrived in the town on horseback. Speeches were made, music played, oxen and sheep were roasted and served to the poor on tables in the High Street. The following evening people danced throughout the night after eating a supper in the Guildhall. The health of the royal family was toasted as the town welcomed their sovereign.

107. Windsor seen from fields near Clewer in about 1803. From a drawing by J. Smith.

George IV upset residents by closing the terraces, except on Sundays. Hitherto, this part of the castle had been open to all and used by children to fly kites or play follow-my-leader. The townspeople were also prevented from taking walks in the Home Park. But George IV's lasting impressions on Windsor are the features he created on the skyline: a refurbished castle with an impressive Round Tower, and a 'Copper Horse' on Snow Hill at the end of the Long Walk.

Before inheriting the throne, George IV had used the Royal Lodge as his Windsor residence. Charles Greville described it as a "delightful place to live", though too small "for very large parties". By then Windsor Castle had little to recommend it as a royal palace without major alterations. Restoration work begun by his father had been suspended during the last 11 years of his life because of the King's failing health, and George IV decided that programme should be revived and considerably expanded.

The House of Commons was approached for a grant and approved a sum of £150,000. Eight commissioners were appointed to ensure that the work was carried out efficiently and economically. In the event, the Commons had little idea how much money and work were involved. Neither had Jeffry Wyatt, nephew of James Wyatt, and chief architect. Perhaps Lord Liverpool had some idea when he drew his pencil across two sides of the plan and said, "You are to go no farther, in the first instance".

Jeffry Wyatt changed his name to Wyatville and received a knighthood shortly after work began. But his estimate of £150,000, which was the sum allowed by the House of Commons, soon proved totally inadequate, particularly as his instructions were to "do everything in a substantial manner, and not merely vamp the building".

Foundations required strengthening, floors needed re-supporting, walls had to be replaced, massive beams renewed, rotten timber made good, and roofs removed and reconstructed with new rafters and lead coverings. Within four years, £400,000 had been spent and a further £244,500 was required to meet the bills in 1828-29. Another £100,000 "that may probably be required in the year" was recommended to Parliament for 1830. Over a million pounds was spent before the work neared completion, undoubtedly excellent value by today's standards, but a huge amount of money in the 1820s.

108. George IV (1820-30).

The question was put to the architect: "Would it have been a greater expense to have taken down the whole building, and used the materials and build a new castle in its stead?" He replied that, since the Middle Ages, the occupants had paid little heed to the building's fabric. Nor was it realised how complex the work would become. When the roof was taken off the living quarters, the opportunity was taken to add a servants' floor. A huge gallery, 550 feet long, to provide access to apartments on the first floor, a suite of offices below, and a new gate for the sovereign to enter into the quadrangle from the Long Walk were just some of the other major undertakings.

Wyatt had to show the Commissioners the rotting timbers supporting the plaster of Verrio's painted ceiling in St George's Hall before they consented to the entire roof being destroyed. This caused an outcry.

Raising the height of the walls of the Round Tower by 33 feet also caused controversy. Purists regard it as a hollow sham, though most agreed the tower's new height gave importance to the keep and created a more impressive image than the earlier squat tower.

In 1902 Murray's *Handbook for Berkshire* stated: "Wyatt professed to preserve the general features of the ancient fortress, and yet to adapt them to the requirements of modern comfort; but the lover of history must regret that the Castle, added to by so many kings, and presenting memorials of so many ages, should be reduced to a state of uniformity. It had, however, been much more maltreated before, and the added height of the Round Tower is a work not less effective than skilful ... but above the skyline is varied and picturesque, and Wyatt is not to be blamed too severely for effacing medieval detail for which little respect was shown before his age, or is shown now."

109. Sir Jeffry Wyatville.

110. Above: Round Tower prior to Wyatville's alterations. From a print c. 1823-24 by W. Wolnoth.

111. Right: Round Tower in Victoria's reign. From a print by Nash.

The Reverend W. Bowles commented: "Windsor Castle loses a great deal of its architectural impression by the smooth neatness with which its old towers are now chiselled and mortared. It looks as if it is washed every morning with soap and water, instead of exhibiting here and there a straggling flower, or creeping weather stains."

In 1951, Sir Owen Morshead wrote: "Even without a bulldozer he did a good deal of damage ... Wyatville was always thinking what Windsor would look like in a wig. He need not have worried. A group of buildings so venerable and so beloved would have looked very well without these meretricious adornments."

In 1957 B. J. W. Hill wrote: "Windsor Castle needs to be seen at a distance; viewed from close, the crenellations, turrets and massive yellow gothic windows of Sir Jeffry Wyatville's Georgian restoration are too bold and overpowering to be beautiful ... When seen with all the battlements and corbels which Wyatville slapped on for good romantic measure, the castle seems to groan beneath its load of stone and sigh for a less heavy-handed architect ... be that as it may, Sir Jeffry found a crumbling ruin and left the nation with a palace."

"We in our day do not like it", wrote A. L. Rowse in 1974, "but it was intended to bind the vast buildings together and elide the variations in the stonework of different periods ... while his raising of the Round Tower by thirty feet was a stroke of genius, which gives a focal point to the whole." Charles II's statue, placed at the centre of the Quadrangle by Tobias Rustat, was given a new position near the Round Tower where it now stands. The Long Walk only came into its modern form when George IV moved buildings which obstructed the view from the Castle. The Queen's Lodge, erected by his father, was one of the buildings which had to go. As a focal point at the far end of the Long Walk, the King planned a massive equestrian statue of George III, dressed in the

112. *South-east view of the apartments in the Upper Ward prior to alterations in the 1820s. From a print by Paul Sandby.*

113. *Similar view to the illustration above painted by Nash in about 1840 and showing Wyatville's alterations.*

regulation Roman toga. He laid the foundation stone for the plinth, but did not live to see the statue erected, nor his work on the castle completed. He died on 26 June 1830 and was buried in St George's Chapel.

Charles Greville wrote: "King George had not been dead three days before everybody discovered that he was no loss ... the breath was hardly out of his body before the press burst forth in full cry against him, and raked up all his vices, follies, and misdeeds". One report said that suppers and parties took place on the night of the funeral and that all of "Windsor was drunk" and showed few signs of grief.

Throughout his life George IV had collected fine paintings, china, furniture and jewellery and, besides his work at Windsor, spared no expense building Brighton Pavilion, remodelling Carlton House, Buckingham Palace and other royal buildings. Earlier the Duke of Wellington had described Prince George and his brothers as "the damnedest millstones about the neck of any government that can be imagined". Later, because of his life style, he was dubbed "the Prince of Pleasure". His subjects were no doubt outraged by his spending, but we who benefit from his cultural legacy should be grateful.

Windsor Castle finally emerged from years of neglect into its modern form, and the 'Copper Horse' became a topic of conversation in the town. One of the horse's legs broke off while the statue was being erected and a huge furnace had to be built to braise it back on. Over a hundred and fifty years later the figure remains a dominant feature on the horizon.

Windsor's population grew to about 5,000 early in the 19th century and it became necessary to enlarge the Guildhall. Mr. Eglestone, the Senior Alderman, laid the foundation stone for the extension in June 1829. Apart from Corporation meetings, the building was in regular use for celebration dinners and fashionable balls, and as a venue for annual meetings of organisations such as the Windsor Horticultural Society, formed in 1827, and weekly lectures by the Windsor and Eton Literary, Scientific and Mechanics' Institute, formed 11 years later.

Gas was introduced to light the streets in 1827 and acclaimed by the *Express* as "decidedly the greatest improvement which has been known for centuries". There were, however, several breakdowns and accidents and Queen Adelaide had the supply to the castle cut off for fear of an explosion.

Towards the end of May 1836 a serious fire began in the cellar of Mr. Ford's house in Thames Street. It burned so fiercely that it consumed Mr. Corbett's hair dressing and perfumery shop next door and set alight windows and shutters on the other side of the street. The army, Ramsbottom's brewery, and the castle sent men and machines to fight the fire, but there was a lack of water and a lot of confusion before the blaze was under control. Three people were unaccounted for until their charred bodies were discovered amongst the ashes.

*115. The Long Walk from
Snow Hill. From a print by
J. D. Harding dated 1840.*

There was a public outcry at the lack of proper facilities to cope with such an event and it took some years before the borough had an organised team of fire fighters. In the 1860s Windsor's "Volunteer Fire Brigade" was established in headquarters in Sheet Street where the Captain, foreman, engineer, honorary officers and 20 pioneers were ready to man a steam fire engine.

XI Beyond the Castle

"At the end of this blackguard heath, you come to a little place called
Sunning Hill, which is on the Western side of Windsor park. It is a
spot all made into grounds and gardens by tax-eaters ".

In February 1665, the diarist Samuel Pepys visited Eton to find "The school
good, and the custom pretty of boys cutting their names in the shuts of the
window when they go to Cambridge". After meeting the boys at class, Dr. Pepys
took some refreshment. "Thence to the porter's, in the absence of the butler, and
did drink of the college beer, which is very good; and went into the back fields
to see the scholars play."

Pepys appears to have enjoyed the college beer which is more than can be
said for Mr. Tucker, who became a common boy (or an Oppidan) at Eton in the
spring of 1811. "I do not think — writing as I do calmly some eighty years after
— that any beverage was ever so vile, villainous, and detestable as the beer
which was put on the three tables in Hall during the time I was in college. It
never improved, never altered. It was brewed on a plan; put into barrels,
worked, and sent up as soon as yeast and fermentation permitted."

116. The Hall, Eton
College, where Mr. Tucker
drank 'vile' beer in the
early 18th century.

117. Eton College seen from the Slough Road.

In 1782, Charles Moritz was on a walking holiday and took the road from Slough to Eton. "I suppose it was during the hour of recreation, or in playtime, when I got to Eton: for I saw the boys in the yard before the college, which was inclosed by a low wall, in great numbers, walking and running up and down.

"Their dress struck me particularly: from the biggest to the least, they all wore black cloaks or gowns, over coloured cloths, through which there was an aperture for their arms. They also wore besides, a square hat or cap, that seemed to be covered with velvet, such as our clergymen in many places wear.

"They were differently employed; some talking together; some playing; and some had their books in their hands, and were reading; but I was soon obliged to get out of their sight, they stared at me so, as I came along, all over dust, with my stick in my hand."

118. First quadrangle, Eton College with Lupton's Tower.

In 1800, Charles Knigh. described Eton as "not very extensive, consisting chiefly of one narrow street, which has within these few years been much improved, by a considerable part of it being paved, and many of the houses rebuilt, or repaired in a neat modern style".

119. Eton High Street.

Much of the surrounding land was still farmed but, as Knight found, subject to flooding. "The overflowing of the Thames here has been more frequent of late, than formerly, owing, as it is supposed, to the prevailing system of canal navigation, as well as to the greater attention that farmers now pay to cleaning their ditches, for the purpose of draining their lands ... Although some temporary inconvenience must arise from these inundations, yet the situation of Eton is thought very healthy, as the waters soon subside, and being on the gravelly soil, the earth soon becomes dry."

120.The Christopher Inn, *Eton.*

Mr. Tucker described his arrival at Eton in 1811. "I was landed from Thumwood's Coach at the 'Christopher', and duly entered the next morning at Keate's Chambers as an Oppidan; was introduced to my Dame, Hawtrey, in Weston's Yard, and left to make my way with some last encouraging words and a farewell pouch. I was just eight and a half years old, and very slender of my age."

Soon after meeting some boys he was enticed into a fight "with a boy of about my own size, but older, to see which was the better man, and then it ended with a genial laugh, and a hand-shake".

Mr. Tucker chose to sleep in the Long Chamber — despite its lack of beds: "... three of us had to sleep on the floor between two bedsteads with heads against the desks. They were decently laid on the adjoining beds during the day time; but as every one had to make his own bed, the floor one bundled down anyhow, trodden on and smirched in the double process of bed-making on each side of it. It was nearly a year — two terms I think — before repeated and strong home complaints brought about a complement of bedsteads. Our generation, perhaps, was less enduring than preceding ones."

A Windsor fair created a diversion for boys in Mr. Tucker's day. "A poor affair, but very decorous. It was chiefly composed of a line of booths from the Town Hall to Castle-yard on one side — the fashionable side, and some scattered booths of a second class on the other, leading towards the Royal Stables. Gingerbread nuts were in the ascendant — a passion of the age in Fair times ... All Windsor and Eton in turn walked solemnly up and down, and made purchases, and trifled with the inevitable nuts. The whole was crowned with a van of wild beasts, and probably with a Giant or a Dwarf."

Another popular attraction was bull-baiting. The poor bull was tethered and a bulldog let loose on it: "... he caught the bull's lip, or he was tossed. In the one he was jerked backwards and forwards in the air until he could hold on no longer, and was thrown into the ring of the sportsmen. In the other he was pitched up high in the air, with perhaps ribs broken or pierced. No matter which; some bets were lost and won, and another dog was set on with some five or ten minutes' delay. And so the sport went on until the sun was nearly down; the bull was then killed, roasted whole, and a merry feast was held on the field lasting far into the morning, amid the most sottish, coarse, and drunken revelry."

By 1858 Tighe and Davis wrote that the college had grown "far beyond the designs of the founder, for her school-rooms are crowded by between six and seven hundred of the wealthiest and most aristocratic families of the land". The college chapel served as the parish church until 1875 when "the increase of the boys at Eton having gradually wedged the townspeople out" resulted in a new church being built. Boys arrived at Eton in ever increasing numbers and in 1891 the total admissions reached a thousand. In fact, numbers became so large, and boys were packed into the college chapel so tightly that some fainted in the crush.

Sunninghill, a hamlet situated in a particularly pleasant part of the forest, developed into a fashionable 18th-century resort. This was partly due to the discovery of 'wells' fed by a spring bearing mineral water. "I have begun to drink Sunninghill waters, which I hope will do me some good", Sarah, Duchess of Marlborough wrote to her granddaughter in June 1734. "They are of the same sort as Tonbridge. And as I take them sometimes at home and sometimes go in my coach to the well, which is exercise and good air, if they do me any good it is vastly better than to go to any of the water places, where there are no tolerable houses to live in." The Duchess was an old lady with a lively mind, but suffered, among other things, from gout. She returned to Marlborough taking bottles of spring water with her, and in August wrote: "I believe Sunninghill waters are much the same as Tonbridge and much more agreeable by being able to take them in one's own house. But I cannot say they have yet done me either good or hurt. For my limbs are weak as they used to be; and I am tormented as much as ever with the itching; which I suppose is the scurvy."

Sunninghill flourished as the belief in the benefits of taking mineral water grew: "... many gentlemen of fortune have here pleasant villas or lodgings for the summer season, to drink the mineral waters, which in many cases are deemed beneficial to health", reported the *Universal Directory of British Trade* in 1796. "The wells are designed with some taste, and are neatly laid out. Assemblies, or public breakfasts, were here held for years past, for the benefit of agreeable conversation, and to partake of the pleasing amusements of this rustic spot." By the 1790s, these assemblies were coming to an end, "meetings have of late been much lessened, but Sunninghill will always be agreeable, and is the residence of many private families".

122. Seventeenth-century Old Wells Inn. *Demolished about 1880. From a drawing by Louisa Wale.*

Robert Triphook, a traveller from Norfolk, came to Windsor in 1805 and described the lonely countryside, much of it common land, between Hungerford Bridge and Windsor: "... that sandy and dreary land known by the name of Bay Heath, nothing is worthy of the traveller's attention ... the same dreary scenery continued after leaving Blackwater, and at Bagshot". Towards Windsor the scenery improved. "The road became more enclosed, and Windsor Park on the left has a most delightful appearance to the eye, after being so long confined to the Barren Heath ... It is almost impossible to conceive the beauty and richness of the woods and scenery which extends on all sides, while the beams of the declining sun, sending its rays on the towers of Windsor Castle, and the surrounding county, contributed to heighten the effect ... We reach Windsor at seven and encamp for the night at the Hope [Frogmore Green], an exceedingly good house at the entrance of the town on the road to Staines."

Another traveller from Norfolk came a few years later. He left a diary but unfortunately no name. He described the scenery between Binfield and Windsor as "... flat and confined by high hedges and trees". He continued: "you have a good view of Winkfield Park and house in passing the road is constantly intersected by cross roads which would be very intricate for a stranger to find out, as you approach Windsor for some miles you see many delightful little cottages and houses planted about with every kind of evergreen shrub laid out in beautiful gardens with gravel walks, you pass close by Virginia Water, every thing here about looks cheerful, could not get accommodation at Windsor and was obliged to drive to Galloway's at the Christopher Inn at Eton, where we found every comfort and accommodation with good bed rooms and moderate charges."

In 1796, Swinley Lodge near Sunninghill was occupied by the master of the buck hounds. His role was to supervise the royal chase, organise hunting parties on behalf of the King and look after the stags and buck hounds. But the days of the chase in Windsor Forest were numbered.

123. Windsor Forest. From a painting by B. West published c. 1801.

A Parliamentary Bill was being discussed to enclose the remaining heaths, commons, moors and wasteland. Landowners saw this as bringing more land into cultivation and some inhabitants believed it was a way of ridding the forest of unruly gangs. Commissioners appointed to administer the scheme met at The *Bells of Ouzeley* on 29 November 1813. Four years later, after many public meetings, discussions and arguments, only small areas of the 'waste' were left for public use. About three quarters were given to private landowners and the Crown received the other quarter. This was attached to the Great Park and detachments of the Royal Horse Guards and Fifth Infantry Regiment spent two days rounding up scattered deer and driving them in. A few months later, the same troops were marching out of Windsor on their way to Belgium to help fight the Battle of Waterloo.

124. Windsor Forest. From a painting by J. Linnell.

William Cobbett, a radical politician and lover of the country, hated the enclosure movement. He wrote in 1822: "On leaving Wokingham for London, you get upon what is called Windsor Forest; that is to say, upon as bleak, as barren, and as villainous a heath as ever man set his eyes on. However, here are new enclosures without end. And here are houses too, here and there, over the whole of this execrable tract of country."

He believed that the Act robbed country folk of their way of life and was concerned about the drift of people away from the villages. "The farm-houses have long been growing fewer and fewer; the labourers' houses have long been growing fewer and fewer; and it is manifest to every man who has eyes to see with, that the villages are regularly wasting away ... The farmhouses are not so many as they were forty years ago by three-fourths. That is to say, the infernal system of Pitt and his followers has annihilated three parts out of four of the farm houses. The labourers' houses disappear also. And all the useful people become less numerous. While these spewy sands and gravel near London are enclosed and built on, good lands in other parts are neglected."

"At the end of this blackguard heath", Cobbett continued, "you come to a little place called Sunning Hill, which is on the Western side of Windsor park. It is a spot all made into grounds and gardens by tax-eaters. The inhabitants of it have beggared twenty agricultural villages and hamlets."

Tighe and Davis were more cautious with their comments about the Inclosure Act. "The forest of Windsor, therefore, no longer exists, although its name is still frequently used, to denote the district south of the Castle. The inclosure of the ground has of course destroyed in a great measure its character."

In 1882, Edward Walford wrote about the area he had known since childhood: "The whole face of the country is now utterly changed". He did, however, find cause for hope. "Although the forest is different from what it was, it is yet a place of rare delight; only a fragment of it, it is true, but a noble one. Once in the forest district and you are at no loss for scenery or objects of beauty and interest. Rough paths lead on every side to some wild woodland solitude, or broad sterile heath, or marsh green with a few osiers, or hilly ridge commanding a rich and various prospect."

With Berkshire's massive growth in the old forest area over the last twenty years, which includes motorways, huge gravel pits, massive housing and industrial estates, and a whole new town at Bracknell, it is difficult to find "wild woodland solitude" today, or get away from continual traffic and aircraft noise.

One positive gain from the Inclosure Act, and a delight for tourist and townspeople of modern Windsor, was the enlargement of the Great Park and further landscaping of Virginia Water. This popular beauty-spot was nothing more than an area of forest waste in the 17th century. It was partially drained in 1623, but remained waste until the Duke of Cumberland, George II's son who defeated the Scots at Culloden, became the Forest Ranger and turned it into a royal playground.

Much of the landscaping is credited to Thomas Sandby, and Sandby's famous artist brother Paul, while the labour force came from Cumberland's own regiment. They used their military training to divert and dam streams which created a vast lake. The Duke had a 50-ton boat hulk hauled overland from the Thames and fitted out as a Mandarin's yacht. When launched, it caused much excitement, "as rich and gay as carving, gilding and japanning could make it".

Disaster came in September 1768 when torrential rain caused a dam to burst, releasing a torrent of water which swept away everything in its path, including a house, "carried off as clean as if no house had ever been built there". The *Annual Register* printed the details: "... the late Duke of Cumberland's fine water-works in Windsor Forest were entirely destroyed; several persons were drowned in different places, as well as houses, oxen, and hogs". Another storm in 1782 caused a similar flood.

Undaunted, the Duke re-established the lake. Dams were rebuilt, thousands of trees planted, the Great West Road diverted, and the village of Harpesford abandoned as it became engulfed by a much larger lake. A new cascade and dam were built using rocks brought from Bagshot Heath.

For a number of years Virginia Water became a royal playground where they enjoyed picnics, boating, fishing, riding and held private celebrations. Later,

King William IV opened up many of the drives through the park for the public
to use as walks, and in the 1930s old boats were removed and derelict cottages
demolished as the whole area became available for public use.

    Another major development came with the appointment of Eric Humphrey
Savill as Deputy Surveyor of the parks and woods in 1931. Sir Eric proposed a
woodland garden near Virginia Water; a suggestion eagerly accepted by
George V. Then, after the Second World War, the Valley Garden was added and
stocked with colourful magnolias, azaleas and rhododendrons. With the addition of another area of garden in 1951, the group became known as the 'Savill
Gardens', in recognition of Eric Savill's work.

*125. Chinese Temple beside
the lake at Virginia Water
from a drawing of about
1840.*

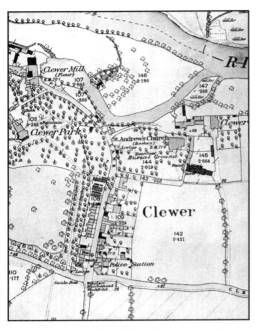

126. In 1881, when this OS map was made, Clewer consisted of a few houses alongside a street leading to the church and the mill.

127. Clewer parish church c. 1820.

128. Clewer mill.

XII   The Widow of Windsor

"The thought of England without the Queen is dreadful even to think of. God help us all!"

129. *Princess Victoria and the Duchess of Kent c. 1834. From an engraving by H. Hayter.*

When a little girl of seven, Victoria visited her uncle, King George IV, and stayed with her aunt, the Duchess of Gloucester, in the Royal Lodge. Later she affectionately wrote: "The King took me by the hand saying, 'Give me your little paw'". George IV was driving his phaeton at Virginia Water when he again met Victoria, "Pop her in", he said, and she was placed beside the King and held tightly by the Duchess, while being driven round the grounds. "(Mamma was much frightened.) I was greatly pleased", Victoria wrote.

In March 1830, when Victoria was aged ten, George IV became ill and had only a few weeks to live. Only then did Victoria realise that her uncle William, who was next in line, stood between her and the throne. Her mother, the Duchess of Kent, had done all she could to prevent Victoria learning of her inheritance. The Princess could not inherit the throne until she was 18, and if uncle William were to die before that date the Duchess would become Regent. Victoria discovered the truth about her birthright by chance, during a history lesson, when looking at a table of the *Kings and Queens of England*. A newly inserted page had brought the royal family tree up to date.

"I never saw that before", exclaimed Victoria.

"No, Princess. It was not thought necessary that you should", replied her governess.

"I am nearer to the throne than I thought."

A few months later, at the age of 65, Victoria's uncle William inherited the throne.

The Princess was discouraged by her mother from visiting Windsor. However, in August 1836, they were both there to celebrate William IV's 71st birthday. They were standing beside him when he made a speech and publicly insulted the Duchess: "I trust in God that my life may be spared for nine months longer, after which period, in the event of my death, no regency would take place." Victoria burst into tears.

It must have been a great relief to the King when, nine months later, Princess Victoria celebrated her 18th birthday. Within a month Victoria was woken by her mother to learn that King William had died at Windsor Castle.

If Windsor Castle, resplendent after its recent refurbishment, was looking for a suitable monarch to occupy its vast apartments, it could have found none more fitting than Queen Victoria. It is almost as if the transformation by George IV had been carried out in preparation for her long reign.

130. *Queen Victoria (1837-1901).*

Windsor Castle as portrayed by Joseph Nash 1840/1844.

131. Lower Ward "on Sunday afternoon".

132. Upper Ward during the arrival of a state visitor by moonlight. A guard of honour stands to attention in the background.

133. Terrace gardens.

134. Christening of Prince Edward (later Edward VII) under the magnificent roof of St George's Chapel, c. 1841.

Queen Victoria hated Windsor Castle at first but grew to love it, and she had an immense influence on the development of the town. She was an independent daughter who listened to the advice of her ministers rather than that offered by her mother. An even greater influence on her young life was Prince Albert, who became her Consort following their marriage in 1840. Prince Albert became involved with a number of activities in the town. He helped found Windsor's Royal Society, and was active in promoting better housing for estate workers and the poor in the town. In Eton he laid the foundation stone of new buildings to accommodate boys who had until then slept in the crowded Long Room.

The Prince established Shaw Farm (or Model Farm) near Frogmore, the Royal Dairy, new fruit and kitchen gardens, and a range of greenhouses 920 feet long. He once told his brother, "I feel as if in paradise in this fine, fresh air". The majority of the trees bordering the Long Walk were elms but Prince Albert, "finding the soil better adapted", planted young oaks as the elms died. By 1945, however, many of these oaks were so badly diseased that they had to be felled and replaced with chestnut and plane.

Though the Prince was respected in many quarters, he was not popular with everyone in Windsor. Local traders complained that his enterprises created unfair competition. Others said that his alterations were done with little respect for their rights or feelings.

Queen Victoria showed considerable interest in her staff. She began a royal school near Cumberland Lodge to educate employees' children and provided money to help with their clothes and lodgings. On occasions, she visited the homes of retired staff to enjoy a chat and an afternoon cup of tea.

136. Queen Victoria and Prince Albert, with their children at play.

The Mayor, Aldermen and Burgesses found themselves regularly called upon to make Addresses of Welcome as Windsor became a mecca for visiting royalty. Emperor Nicholas I of Russia, Leopold I, King of the Belgians, and King Louis Philippe of France came in 1844, while Napoleon III and Victor Emmanuel, King of Sardinia, arrived on state visits in 1855.

With horse power still the main form of propulsion, new stables were built at a discreet distance from the castle to house 100 horses and 40 carriages, landaus, phaetons and garden chairs. An indoor riding school, 165 feet long, completed the plan. Houses in Thames Street, which had encroached on the castle ditch, were purchased and demolished. The last to be pulled down stood at the foot of the Hundred Steps. Tighe and Davis knew it well. "The gable-ended front, the upper part overhanging the lower, with the little low-roofed shop, made it so fitting a specimen of the street architecture of medieval times as to deserve a slight passing notice. The antique house was the property of the Dean and Canons of St George's Chapel, one of the lay-clerks occupying it, whose office was to lock and unlock the doors of the Hundred Steps."

Tighe and Davis also wrote of an old solution being re-introduced to supply water to the castle in 1850. "A constant and full supply of water to all parts of the castle had been secured by laying down pipes to the interior of the castle from a reservoir near Winkfield."

In the mid-19th century, poor drainage was still a prime cause of death. Typhoid, diarrhoea and cholera infected rich and poor alike. The poor were housed in cheap dwellings crowded together on low-lying ground with no running water or sanitation. Much sewerage ended up in the Thames, and as a result of the river overflowing in 1852 houses in Bier Lane (now perhaps more appropriately called River Street) had flood water mixed with sewage flowing into living rooms and kitchens for up to 17 days.

Six years later, the Court Physician declared that typhoid fever had reached epidemic proportions in Windsor. Queen Victoria wrote "it cannot be denied that there is room for improvement for house drainage ... our town is far from being perfect".

One of Prince Albert's last engagements took him to Eton in December 1861 when Queen Victoria presented colours to the College Rifle Volunteers. He was only 42 but looked much older and was obviously very ill. Doctors diagnosed typhoid fever, and medical theory today suggests that it was complicated by cancer.

Shortly after the Eton visit the surgeon, Henry Brown, told Queen Victoria that Albert's health was improving: "I think there is ground to hope that the crisis is over", he said. The Queen went to the Prince's room. "It was a bright morning, the sun just rising and shining brightly. The room had the sad look of night-watching, the candles burnt down to their sockets, the doctors looked anxious. I went in, and never can I forget how beautiful my darling looked, lying there with his face lit up by the rising sun, his eyes unusually bright, gazing as it were on unseen objects, and not taking notice of me." She was devastated that evening when given the news that he had died.

137. Wolsey's Chapel received elaborate decoration when it was converted into a Memorial Chapel for Prince Albert.

138. Edward, Prince of Wales, with his bride-to-be proceeding along Eton High Street ...

Queen Victoria withdrew almost completely from public life. When the Prince of Wales brought his beautiful bride-to-be to Windsor in March 1863, after a brief conversation with the couple the Queen retired to her lonely room. "Strangers arrive, and he, my beloved one, not be there", she wrote.

Dressed in black, in deep mourning, Queen Victoria sat alone in St George's Chapel, during the marriage service, surrounded by gorgeous uniforms and colourful gowns. As the wedding guests celebrated, she drove to Frogmore to pray at her husband's tomb.

The Queen found some comfort in her large and ever growing family as children, grandchildren, and great-grandchildren tried to console her.

The public eventually began to resent paying taxes for a sovereign who appeared to do very little in return. A new generation was growing up which prompted *The Times* newspaper to print that Victoria should "show herself to the present generation which knows her not".

By then Britain was extending its Empire, and Prime Minister Disraeli astutely secured for Victoria the title Empress of India.

The Queen disliked London, and Windsor was the nearest residence to the capital that she would use. Under her, the town virtually took over Westminster's role as everybody of importance came for audience in the castle. Ambassadors arrived from all parts of the world to pay homage. Indian princes laid swords at her feet and declared their loyalty. Colourful natives played strange instruments and danced, almost naked, to entertain her on the terraces. Priceless gifts were presented and pledges of devotion and allegiance given.

As Britain's prosperity and influence grew, so people warmed to Queen Victoria. Her popularity and influence increased to such an extent that some believed she personally had created the Empire. Eton college played its role in national affairs as boys were educated to become statesmen, lawyers, military leaders, and country gentlemen. Many were in Windsor to form a torchlight procession in 1897, when the Queen's Diamond Jubilee was celebrated.

139. ... while the Mayor and Corporation of Windsor wait at the foot of Thames Street to present an Address of Welcome.

Queen Victoria reigned for 64 years and many of her subjects had known no other monarch. She died at Osborne in 1901 and her body was brought to Windsor by train for burial in the mausoleum next to that of Prince Albert. At the Great Western Station, the coffin was placed on a gun-carriage and the leading band, playing the 'Death March', moved off towards Castle Hill. At that moment a calamity occurred when the leading horse drawing the gun-carriage reared and broke the harness. The band had to be stopped and chaos overtook those at the station. Gunners tried to patch the broken straps and Prince Louis of Battenberg suggested that the naval guard should pull the gun-carriage. The artillerymen protested but stood aside as the sailors removed the horses, picked up the harnesses and hauled the carriage in procession towards St George's Chapel.

Only after thorough testing of harnesses, and a number of careful rehearsals, were the gunners allowed to convey the Queen's body from St George's Chapel for burial in the mausoleum.

140. Queen Victoria's funeral procession makes its way across the Upper Ward for the mausoleum at Frogmore. Ever since her interment the navy has retained the privilege of drawing the gun-carriage at a sovereign's funeral.

The sad scene was described in a small tourist's guide book a few months later. "Resting on a gun-carriage drawn by eight horses ... the coffin was borne through the precincts of the Castle and down the Long Walk, many thousands of spectators lining the route. King Edward VII followed immediately after the coffin, the German Emperor coming next. Queen Alexandra led the procession of royal ladies, while the young Prince Edward of York walked by her side. The start and progress of the procession was marked by the firing of 15-pounder guns in the Long Walk, and the tolling of the Mausoleum bell, answered by the great bell of the Round Tower.

"Beyond the entrance to the grounds of Frogmore the ceremonial was private. The Committal Prayer was read by the Bishop of Winchester, and the soil — understood to have been brought from the Holy Land — was cast upon the coffin by Lord Edward Pelham-Clinton, Master of her late Majesty's Household."

Queen Victoria saw the dawn of a new century, and her death signalled the end of an era. People had become so used to her being there that Princess May must have summed up the country's feelings when she said: "The thought of England without the Queen is dreadful even to think of. God help us all!"

141. As part of the celebrations for the Jubilee in 1887 a statue of Queen Victoria, standing on a granite pedestal, was placed on Castle Hill. The Queen watched as Prince Christian, High Steward of Windsor, unveiled the figure.

XIII   Victorian Inheritance

"The distance from London to Slough, eighteen miles, was accomplished in very little more than half an hour, and at Slough other royal carriages were in waiting, in order to convey us rapidly through the small and ancient Town of Eton to the palace of Windsor".

It is easy to criticise the Victorian age and judge it with our 20th-century values, particularly as it fostered ideals which modern thinking has completely swept away. But in Windsor, as in many British towns, the Victorians left a legacy which affects our lives in many ways even today. One of the most important tangible assets of this inheritance is railways. Victorian roads were generally in poor condition and travelling by coach was slow, and could involve hardship and danger. Roads had improved little from early times when bad weather often caused serious delays. On occasions coaches became wedged in snowdrifts and passengers froze to death. Floods covering the road at Egham in December 1768 were so severe that the Exeter coach was overturned and all the occupants drowned. A post-chaise belonging to William Clode of the *White Hart*, Windsor, was returning from Egham in February 1814 with a passenger when the postilion decided to give the horses a rest. He drove the carriage into the Thames near the *Bells of Ouzeley*, intending to wash both horses and carriage. But the water was running swifter and deeper than he thought and they were soon in trouble. The passenger could not swim and realised the danger. He climbed out of the window and onto the roof. From there he leaped to the bank. The postilion attempted to control the horses but the animals were soon drowned. He was pulled from the water by amazed onlookers. There is no record of what the landlord of the *White Hart* said to the driver, but the horses and carriage were found next day nine miles down-river.

Even if passengers did arrive safely, they often found the journey slow and tiring. Charles Knight recalls travelling to London with his father early in the 19th century when the journey "was satisfactorily performed in the usual time of five hours, and a little more". In 1815 one guide book proclaimed that the coach journey between London and Windsor had been cut from ten to less than four hours. By 1836 the fastest mail coach from London to Bristol took 11 hours.

When the idea of railways was introduced, the natural step was to fit coaches and carriages with iron wheels suitable for running on rails. One proposal in 1833 suggested that horses should be used to pull coaches on a railway between Colnbrook and Windsor, with a terminal near Clewer church. But even though steam engines were noisy and polluted the air, it soon became obvious that horses were not suitable for pulling railway carriages.

Were entrepreneurial engineers such as Joseph Locke and Isambard King-dom Brunel attempting such projects today, they would find planning restrictions, rising costs, and the objections of environmentalists almost impossible to overcome. But even in the 1830s, there were powerful pressure groups active in Windsor and laying the tracks was not easy. Objections came from those with vested interests such as river traders and coach operators who feared that their jobs were in jeopardy. The Crown held most of the land and was reluctant to release it, while Eton College was able to put up a powerful lobby. The Provost believed that the boys would be in danger and said he would be criminally wanting in duty if he did not declare that a railway would be ruinous to the school. He made it clear that the college would endeavour to prevent a line being built.

When Brunel's Great Western Railway began operating from Paddington in 1838, the idea of a line to Windsor had been dropped, partially due to the Provost's objections. The college also delayed construction of a station at Slough and passengers for the area had to buy tickets at the *Crown Hotel* or the *North Star* public house. Eton College finally gave way in 1840 and Slough got its station.

142. Queen Victoria and Prince Albert in a royal train with Louis Philippe, King of France, during a state visit.

In June 1842, Queen Victoria travelled from Slough to Paddington in a special train and no doubt realised that she was at the dawn of a new age in transport. Important foreign dignitaries came and sampled the revolutionary railway. In 1844, Doctor Carus, physician to the King of Saxony, accompanied the entire entourage on a rail journey from Paddington to Windsor. "The distance from London to Slough, eighteen miles, was accomplished in very little more than half an hour, and at Slough other royal carriages were in waiting, in order to convey us rapidly through the small and ancient town of Eton to the palace of Windsor. As we passed by the college of Eton, founded by Henry VI, the boys were drawn up in front of this ancient Gothic edifice, most of them dressed in black, but some in scarlet coats, and welcomed the King of Saxony and saluted the Queen with a hearty hurrah."

Railways were a huge success and day trips from London to Windsor became feasible. Edward Jesse was one of the first writers to promote such a trip. "We will land our visitor at Slough, after he has passed along a portion of the Great Western Railway, unrivalled as it is for the smoothness and rapidity with which we travel along it — its punctuality — its arrangements — its comparative safety — the great civility of its attendants and the stupendous cost of its works, which no other country but this could perhaps have undertaken."

On busy days hundreds of passengers took Mr. Jesse's advice and travelled by train to Slough. They arrived in Windsor by omnibus, coach, horse or on foot, and this caused a constant stream of traffic to pass through Eton and, as college buildings occupied both sides of the road, through the college itself.

Pressure was applied by the railway companies and businessmen and it became obvious that a rail link to Windsor would have to be built. Several ideas to overcome objections were advanced. One involved constructing new centres to house Windsor's and Eton's population well away from the castle and college. Windsor would be built on a grid system with a central square, and Eton would have a new main street. They would be connected by a new bridge crossing the Thames near Clewer church and trains were to pass through a tunnel dug under the Long Walk, before emerging in New Windsor.

These plans were rejected and the Great Western and the South-Western rail companies put forward individual proposals. Opinion in Eton and Windsor was divided; some thought one rail was sufficient. The *Express* acclaimed the merits, or condemned the drawbacks, of various schemes, and noisy meetings were held in the Town Hall. The Corporation and traders saw the advantage of direct communications with the rest of the country, and the military in the speedy movement of troops. Appeals were made to the Crown to release necessary land, and arguments to counter the college's objections were put forward.

In 1847, the basis of a deal was struck in which the South-Western Company agreed to pay £60,000 "towards the expense of constructing the said roads and bridges, and of widening and improving Thames Street and High Street". The station was to use the names of both Eton and Windsor, have 14 large doors for the use of the Cavalry, and a private entrance for the Queen.

143. The South-Western railway reaches Windsor. From a print published by A. B. Brown in about 1851.

144. Great Western station. From a print published by A. B.Brown in about 1851.

In August of the following year, the Great Western Company also received the go-ahead and paid £25,000 for about thirteen acres of Crown land at Eton and one and a quarter in Windsor to accommodate line and station. This, too, was to have accommodation for Her Majesty.

The agreements were seen by *The Gentleman's Magazine*, which appears to have been years ahead of its time in considering the environment, as an ideal settlement. "One good consequence of rail-roads is that they render mere turnpike and common road 'improvements', which were often made at the sacrifice of natural beauties, less requisite than before. In the present instance, the rail-roads have both suggested and, owing to the hard bargain of the Commissioners of Woods, have actually supplied the funds for the improvement of the ordinary roads."

When the Great Western's line from Slough finally crossed the Thames by "a handsome bow bridge" to the station in George Street, it could have been argued that railway passengers were in danger from the boys of Eton — rather than the other way round, as the Provost feared. "At the baths near the Great Western Railway Bridge", wrote an observant passenger, "a young fellow stood on the bank in perfect nakedness, and as the train arrived opposite the baths, instead of retiring ... he faced round to the train with a leering laugh."

A more serious event involved Queen Victoria when she was leaving the station in March 1882. A man named Maclean tried to shoot her but he fortunately missed and was seized by a local called Burnside, helped by two boys from Eton. It was the sixth attempt made on her life.

Some visitors, such as Doctor Carus, enjoyed a private view of Victoria's castle. "When the hour for retiring arrived, I went alone through the series of magnificent apartments and the long richly-adorned gallery, with its numerous interesting paintings, to my own solitary chamber. Everything was still brilliantly lighted — what riches everywhere displayed! Immense malachite vases,

golden candelabra, the splendour of the furniture and draperies, the large golden vessel,
like a small bath, which was filled with spiced
wine at the baptism of the Prince of Wales,
and entirely emptied; the glass cases filled
with ancient splendid weapons, swords,
chain armour, beautifully ornamented
pistols, guns and daggers." The doctor was
indeed privileged. Early Victorian guide
books informed visitors: "The Private Apartments occupy the eastern end of the castle,
and are not shown to the public".

With the growing network of railways,
faster trains and cheaper travel, it became
possible for ordinary people from as far away

*145. Silver-gilt wine-cooler
used at Royal Christening.*

as the Midlands and Northern counties to enjoy a day excursion and see
Windsor Castle for themselves. Those who braved the Hundred Steps, which
provided a short cut from the riverside station to the Lower Ward, found them
something of an effort. "They are somewhat fatiguing to ascend", tourists were
warned. But Walford's guide thought the climb was worth the effort; the north
terrace was particularly rewarding: "... the finest walk of its kind in England,
should be visited for the sake of the magnificent prospects it commands. The
spectator stands in the centre of a panorama of unequalled beauty." Today much
of the view from the terrace is hidden behind a canopy of trees.

Visitors were recommended to see the parks. "The Home Park, adjoining the
Castle, contains 400 acres, and is about four miles in circumference. It is studded
everywhere with stately avenues of elms and groups of the finest trees, amongst
them being some magnificent oaks."

One old oak was named after Herne the Hunter, a legendary character of
Windsor Forest immortalised in Shakespeare's *Merry Wives of Windsor*. The fate
of Herne's Oak itself became a matter of mystery and speculation. Some
believed the tree blew down in strong winds on August 1863, but Murray's
handbook expressed doubts: "A withered and barkless oak, enclosed by a
railing, long stood in the line of the avenue of elms, and bore the name of *Herne's
Oak* ... though it is more probable that the real tree was accidentally cut down
by George III, in 1796." Mr. Perry, woodcarver to Queen Victoria, used wood
from the tree which had succumbed in the gale to carve mementoes and testified
that it had indeed been from Herne's Oak. Queen Victoria replaced the fallen
oak with a sapling, thus ensuring that the legend would continue.

James Edmund Vincent stayed at the *White Hart* hotel in about 1880, "then
an old fashioned inn", and witnessed what he called the "nightly parliament,
quite informal, of the civic worthies of Windsor". Was the affluence of the town
going to these people's heads? Vincent certainly gave that impression when he
accused them of being "more pompous, than that of their equals in station in
the average provincial town. These very considerable tradesmen, perhaps they
were warrant-holders, seemed to set themselves up as superior to others of their
class".

146. Harriet Monsell (Mother Monsell) in 1786, at the age of 28. She was the main founder of the House of Mercy in Clewer.

Attractions pointed out by Victorian guide books included "a red-bricked house, built by order of Charles II for Nell Gwynne and her son, the Duke of St Albans." And "an obelisk, erected in 1810 in memory of George III", built on the old public recreation ground at Bachelor's Acre. Even Windsor's new barracks were on the list: "... extensive barracks for both infantry and cavalry. The former, situate in Sheet Street, contains accommodation for 1000 men; the Cavalry Barracks, in Spital Road, have accommodation for about the same number." These were built to replace older barracks, condemned when the sanitary commissioners reported amongst other problems: "... there was not a single urinal which did not stink abominably". In 1864, Queen Victoria was horrified when she saw the squalor in which the troops lived.

Being a garrison town, beer houses and brothels were commonplace. In 1860 there were seven beer houses and four houses of ill repute in Clewer Lane alone. These attracted uneducated girls from desperately poor families who become prostitutes. For many it was the only means of earning a living.

Mrs. Tennant, the widow of a clergyman, provided shelter for some of these girls at a house called 'The Limes' near Clewer church. She was forced to give up the work because of poor health in 1851 but the movement she founded grew under the guidance of Harriet Monsell, into 'The House of Mercy' the home of the Clewer Sisters.

The sanitary conditions in Windsor were disgraceful. Several official reports condemned the Corporation for its apathy and a leading councillor was accused of being more interested in scarlet robes than his tenants. The Board of Health was persuaded to construct a system of underground sewers which, by 1875,

147. In 1875, an artist for The Illustrated London News *discovered how ingenious the people of Windsor were at coping with flooding.*

148. *Delivering coal to houses near the gas works during the 1875 floods.*

were feeding effluent to a treatment works on Ham Island in Old Windsor. But the town still retained large areas of slums. While the Industrial Revolution was building Britain's empire and creating employment and wealth in many parts of England, little industry was created in Windsor. Employment at the castle, two breweries, an aerated water factory, or domestic service, were the main options for those seeking work.

Stressing the town's affluent side, *Dutton's Directory* placed Windsor "in the centre of an extensive district containing many mansions and estates of the nobility and gentry: within several miles are upwards of 100 seats". *Kelly's Directory* also noted an aura of prosperity. "For the supply of the many wealthy residents and visitors the town has establishments and shops of a higher class than are usually met with in a place of this size." There followed a long list of 'Private Residents', demonstrating Windsor's attractions as a fashionable place to live.

The parish church was described as "a spacious building, of poor modern architecture, and somewhat plain in its exterior". However, the 'spacious building' was not able to cope with the population which virtually doubled in the 19th century. Canon Ellison also realised that rents charged for pews made seating in the church too expensive for the town's poor. He began a fund for a new church — All Saints — which would provide free seating, and Queen Victoria donated £300 towards the costs. Her daughter, Victoria, Crown Princess of Prussia, laid the foundation stone in 1863 and a year later, along with numerous members of the Household, attended the opening ceremony. Other denominations also required new places of worship. A Catholic church, dedicated to Edward the Confessor, opened in October 1868, Holy Trinity in Trinity Place was erected 1842-3, and St Saviour's, a chapel of ease to Holy Trinity, in 1876.

The Albert Institute in Sheet Street was opened by Edward, Prince of Wales, in January 1881 to provide the town with reading rooms, billiard tables, special rooms for ladies, class rooms, a library with between 3,000 and 4,000 books, a lecture hall to seat 500, and a museum. Other entertainment was provided when horse races were organised on private land beside the Thames at Clewer in 1865. This proved a success and plans were made to hold annual meetings, and build a grandstand.

The June races at Ascot were popular with the Prince and Princess of Wales and royal guests. Doctor Carus described the scene in 1884 which, apart from the mode of transport, has changed little. "It was towards one o'clock when we drove to Ascot races. These are among the most celebrated in England, and to-day the Queen's plate was to be run for ... Soon after we had left the park and approached the race-course, the number of carriages and riders increased; at length the vast heath with its various roads opened upon me, which was already covered with a vast number of persons. Amidst loud cheering the court, in fourteen carriages, drove along the race-course to the pavilion specially erected for the Queen ... There were perhaps from 25,000 to 30,000 persons present. These took up their positions, partly on both sides of the course, partly in various houses and on scaffolding. A number of policemen were employed in keeping order. Round about were masses of tents, and numbers of carriages covered with human beings. Thimble-riggers and gypsies were not wanting. Among the spectators were a great many ladies and people of the best ton. The place itself is to a certain extent waste, really a heath, here and there stony; all this presented a remarkable picture under a greyish, rainy-looking sky."

By the end of the century, electric light was brightening Windsor's skies from a dynamo fitted to a 10-horse-power engine in the *White Hart* hotel. A shop in Peascod Street also had electricity installed in 1892. Soon afterwards the Windsor and Eton Electric Light Company was laying cables to other premises in Peascod Street, High Street and Thames Street.

The telegraph reached Windsor in 1849. "The Electric Fluid travels at the rate of 280,000 Miles per Second", declared a handbill. But the first practical telephone was invented in 1876 by the American, Alexander Graham Bell. Two years later he visited Britain to promote the apparatus and presented Queen Victoria with two telephones in ivory. Many people rejected such contraptions and a telephone exchange was not built in Windsor until 1891. Three years later only five subscribers were listed in the directory.

Toll charges on the Windsor Bridge were a cause for controversy towards the end of Victoria's reign. Earlier, in 1819, Parliament authorised the Council to collect the payments for a period of 21 years to help fund the then new bridge. By 1895 Joseph Taylor, an Eton Urban District Councillor, declared that the debt had been well and truly cleared. He regarded the tolls as illegal and began a campaign to have them suspended. After paying his twopence to cross the bridge in January 1896, he issued a writ to recover the money. It took nearly three years of legal wrangling before the House of Lords declared that toll collecting on Windsor Bridge was unlawful. Mr. Husteds, the toll-keeper, whose family had held the right for nearly forty years, and had paid the Corporation about £27,000 for the privilege, saw the gates and posts come down and his livelihood disappear.

XIV Windsor in Wartime

"The die has been cast and England is at war with Germany".

Windsor played such a prominent role in Britain's Empire at the beginning of this century that Albert Lee, a Windsor historian, was prompted to write: "The palace may be looked upon as the centre of the Empire, and in a sense the centre of the world ... none can vie with this magnificent castle on Windsor's mound. For here one reads the story of a nation coming out of compactness of an Empire, the like of which the world has never seen before."

149. View of Windsor from the Great Western Railway in about 1910. From a painting by E. W. Haslehust.

James Vincent, who knew the town from earlier visits, noted the changes. "Near the Town Hall are some nice old houses (to look at, not to inhabit), and a few in Peascod Street. Not a vestige remains of the inns that Falstaff and, as we need not doubt, the creator of Falstaff, knew full well ... the White Hart is, from an aesthetic point of view, sadly modern, having been completely rebuilt at some time, probably quite recent." The rebuilt hotel opened in 1889 and Nikolaus Pevsner described it as "lifted straight out of Kensington".

"It is a hotel, however, at which man may stay in reasonable comfort", continued Mr. Vincent, "though there are London hotels where more comfort can be secured for less money. They have not, however, as the *White Hart* has, a full view of the Castle Hill." Rooms overlooking the castle were at a premium, particularly during great ceremonial events. "In truth, to sit on a balcony of the *White Hart* on such occasions, in delicious scorn of the crowd jostling on the pavement beneath, is to enjoy the sensations of one in the Royal Box at the theatre."

In 1902, John Murray expressed disappointment at the loss of his favourite view: "... the most characteristic and medieval impression was formerly obtained from the far end of the departure platform of the old G W R station, until the group of admirably built red houses was disfigured by corrugated iron and lofty new erections."

150. *Church Street looking towards Henry VIII's Gate in about 1908. From a painting by M. Henton.*

151. *Looking down Church Street towards the parish church and the* Ship Commercial Hotel. *From a painting by M. Henton.*

Murray was also very concerned about how the rest of the town was developing. "There are some beautiful 17th-century houses in Church Street between the Vicarage and the Town Hall; but they are deplorably neglected, and commonplace building has supplanted many old houses in the High Street which had tiled roofs and excellent interiors. The last good house (The Cedars), in Peascod Street, has been destroyed, and few suburbs are less attractive than those which have grown up round this splendid medieval centre."

In February 1911, a memorable occasion took place when King George V and Queen Mary were at Windsor to congratulate Thomas Sopwith on winning £4,000 for the longest flight in Britain in a British aircraft. After their Coronation at Westminster the following June, the royal couple returned to Windsor and part of their schedule was to review the Territorials, the Eton College Volunteers and the Boy Scouts. In September the first aerial postal service in England was initiated when the King's mail came to Windsor by aeroplane, the pilot having special permission to land in a meadow near Shaw Farm.

152. Peascod Street in about 1908. From a painting by M. Henton.

153. Second Life Guards on church parade in about 1912.

154. Caffyn's Corner.
From a pencil drawing by
James P. Power.

The editor of the *Express* summed up 1913 as a year of advancement for the country, but thought Windsor should have been more prosperous. Crowds had visited the town in large numbers, using newly introduced motor buses, but the Court had been in residence for only a few weeks and the State Apartments were closed to the public. This was to counter the threat that militant members of the suffragette movement would vandalise the rooms.

But prospects looked better for 1914. There were bargains on offer at the annual sales held by Herbert's supply store in Eton, and Caley's in Windsor. Splendid performances of Gilbert and Sullivan's *Yeomen of the Guard* were being given by the Royal Albert Institute Operatic and Dramatic Society, *Little Red Riding Hood* attracted crowds to the Theatre Royal, and the Mayor had approached the authorities with the result that the State Apartments were to be re-opened. Perhaps the best news came from the Town Hall where the Councillors were discussing a reduction in the rates of five pence in the pound.

When the royal party arrived in late January 1914, the *Express* reported a large crowd assembled to welcome them and all were pleased to see the castle occupied again. The coming and going of royal carriages, and the band of the Coldstream Guards playing as they daily marched to the castle "causes our streets to assume a lively air", reported the paper. It was pleased to announce: "some of our traders too will have a busy time with the Court here".

The paper's letter column reflected the worries of the day with "Home rule for Ireland", top of the list. Close second came arguments about Windsor's cinemas being allowed to open on Sundays. The Wesleyan community deplored the move and the Council appealed to the management to show suitable films only. Some said the Lord's Day was a day of rest, others replied that people were indeed resting when they were in a cinema. One writer was pleased that the "Peoples Electric Theatre" had decided not to open, and hoped the other two cinemas would follow its example.

The *Express* was congratulated for its reporting of a talk by Mr. Philip Snowden on "The case for womens Suffrage". The writer suggested a local branch be formed to support the national movement. But the crusade was creating local problems; within a few weeks the paper announced a "blow to Windsor" with the closure once again of the State Apartments. This was brought on by an "outrage" in the National Gallery, blamed on the suffragettes. Voices rose in indignation "at the doing of these militant women". Later articles accused the suffragettes of causing fires which destroyed a house called 'The Willows', near Windsor, and Wargrave church.

Earlier, the Mayor had made it clear while speaking at a dinner in which a number of women were present, that he was pleased to be in the company of ladies. He told the guests that they had much greater freedom now and were occupying positions previously held by men. It was even acceptable for them to ride bicycles, and no notice was taken of women riding side saddle; "public opinion was changing with regard to the fair sex". The Mayor went so far as to suggest that ladies should be invited to the annual Mayoral Banquet and Venison Dinner.

155. Advertisement for the Royal Windsor Cycle Company.

Wages were low and Eton Council decided to follow Windsor and Slough's example by increasing roadmen's pay by 2d. per week. Some were earning as little as £1. The *Express* regarded this as inadequate: "... a wage of twenty-five shillings would not be too liberal".

There was no shortage of places to drink, even though a number of public houses and clubs had been closed. There remained one licensed house available for every 150 inhabitants. Crime figures had steadily increased over the previous eight years; 98 offences were reported in 1913, and 51 people were proceeded against. Of those, only 25 had been local residents.

Increased use of motor transport caused major concern. Many roads were unsurfaced and people complained that passing traffic filled their houses with dust. As a remedy, 30,000 gallons of tar were obtained to spray on the town's streets. One stretch of roadway in the Great Park between Queen Anne's Gate and Ascot was in a particularly bad condition and cyclists and pedestrians protested at being driven off the roads by so many motor cars. The weight of vehicles led to fears about the safety of the Victoria and Albert bridges which had not been designed for such traffic. The Albert Bridge was said to be "most defective". Experts were called in to report and councillors argued about finding the money, but they need not have worried. When repairs were carried out on Victoria Bridge in 1968, British Rail discovered that a clause in the original agreement between the Crown and the railways held the companies responsible for maintenance.

A very close link had been formed between Princess Christian and the town and, to complement the work she had done for charities, the Corporation decided that 4 June 1914 should be

156. Catering for the cyclists in Peascod Street. From a drawing by Fred Richards.

celebrated by a 'floral fete' and called 'Helena Day'. The *Express* was full of praise for the continual support she had given to the Nursing and Maternity Homes and King Edward VII's Hospital. To mark the day, the streets were decorated with flags and a 21-gun salute fired in the Long Walk. There is "no better Princess in the land", said the Mayor, and nearly 90,000 roses were sold in the street to raise money for charities. The weather was perfect but the day was marred because the Princess was ill, and not able to attend.

King George V found time in his busy schedule to fire a gun outside the castle to start the annual marathon to London. Twenty-six miles later, Djebelia, a 17-year-old 'Arab', running for a French club, led the field.

157. Start of the Polytechnic Marathon Race from Windsor to Stamford Bridge.

In August 1914, the peaceful life of England was shattered when the country declared war on Germany. The *Express* announced the news in its editorial: "The die has been cast and England is at war with Germany". Successive editions reported the town's preparations and praised the Clewer Horticultural Society for its initiative on advising allotment holders, and those with spare land, to sow turnip and turnip rooting beetroot in readiness for food shortages.

People crowded into the Town Hall to hear news of plans which had been made. Men who had passed their prime, but were still willing to serve the country, were invited to volunteer for the Civil Guard. Those who were fit were urged to enlist at a recruiting office set up in the Town Hall. Shoppers were recommended to support local traders whose businesses were bound to suffer from lack of trade.

On hearing the news, the vicar of Windsor immediately returned from holiday, as men were mobilised in the barracks and recruits arrived to fill the regiments. Clewer Park was placed at the disposal of the Red Cross, and the stands at Ascot turned into a hospital for wounded soldiers. Windsor races were abandoned, and the police combed the area to confiscate horses urgently needed by the cavalry. A number of Germans living in the area were arrested, and German-made toys taken out of shop windows and removed from the shelves.

On 29 August crowds lined the street to cheer, wave flags and handkerchiefs, and give the Coldstream Guards a good send-off. The men sang patriotic songs as they marched from Victoria Barracks to the South Western Station. Last goodbyes were said as the troops boarded the train. As the engine steamed out of the station and the last carriage disappeared from view, the crowds returned home believing the war would soon be over.

Within a few days, the Coldstream Guards were in action and reports began to reach Windsor of how bravely they were fighting. A number of German attacks had been resisted at Compiègne, Soissons and by the River Aisne. But casualties were heavy on both sides and many men would not return home. Captain Charles Hunter Browning of the Royal Field Artillery, and prospective Liberal candidate for Windsor, was one of the first casualties reported killed in the Battle of Mons.

The Archbishop of Canterbury and Lord Kitchener made an appeal asking well-wishers not to treat soldiers who were leaving for the trenches to too much alcohol. "We trust it will be respected to in this district", the *Express* wrote. "In Windsor the scenes in the streets have not been at all creditable on one or two occasions, and the effects on the soldiers are not good", the paper continued. "Another subject that is worth mentioning is the behaviour of many young girls in the town. They hang around the barrack gates, and run after the soldiers in a way that is most unbecoming." A few days later the magistrates decided that all licensed premises were to close one hour earlier.

The great topic of conversation in November centred on the large number of soldiers who arrived in the town and required billeting. Homes were found in the area for 5,000 men, but how to entertain them during the long dark evenings remained a problem. The Mayor placed the Corn Exchange, under the Town Hall, at the disposal of the military authorities, and local organisations responded to appeals for help and organised a variety of entertainments.

The suffragette movement shelved their activities for the duration and achieved a certain amount of equality. They became vital recruits for women's regiments and filled vacancies left in shops, offices, factories and farms by enlisted men.

As the war dragged on, casualties rose to so much that virtually every family in the country suffered the loss of at least one close relative. As men reached 18 they were enlisted, and casualties became so high that the upper age limit for recruitment was raised to 50 for certain categories of men. The war was going against the Allies and anti-German feeling surged almost to fever pitch. London shops, whose owners had German names, were looted and the King reluctantly agreed that the banners in St George's Chapel of eight enemy rulers and princes, who were Knights of the Garter, should be taken down.

Because of King George V's ancestry and concern over his family name, some believed that he must be pro-German. Amongst the majority of his people, there was absolutely no doubt of George V's loyalty, particularly in Windsor. But when Lord Stamfordham proposed that King George V might adopt the name Windsor, the idea was accepted. The House of Windsor came into being on 17 July 1917. A new dynasty had begun and, with it, a lasting bond between the monarchy and the borough.

158. George V (1910-36) photographed amidst the desolation after the fighting at Wytschaete Ridge in 1917.

XV   Freedom of Windsor

*"This town, whose name my family bears, is very dear to me. Indeed,
I regard it as home in a way no other place can be". (Her Majesty the
Queen, on receiving the Honorary Freedom of the Royal Borough in
1947)*

Edward VIII succeeded to the throne in January 1936, but abdicated the follow-
ing December in favour of his brother Prince Albert. On succession, Prince
Albert preferred to use his last Christian name and was known as King
George VI (1936-52). He created his brother Edward the Duke of Windsor, and
began the task of heading a nation which was soon to be engulfed in the Second
World War.

When the conflict broke, Windsor Castle was regarded as a comparatively
safe haven, as its massive walls and dungeon-like rooms offered almost total
protection from bombing. The crown jewels were wrapped in newspaper and
placed in the castle vaults and Windsor became a permanent home for Princess
Elizabeth and Margaret.

Both took active roles in local life. They performed in plays with children
from the Park School and helped to raise funds for the war effort. They became
accomplished pianists and enthusiastic Girl Guides. Princess Margaret joined
the Sea Rangers and Princess Elizabeth was taught to ride at the Royal Lodge
by Henry Owen, the King's groom. She also joined the ATS to become a transport
driver. Before Princess Elizabeth was fully proficient, she stalled a heavy lorry
while driving in Windsor. "What do you think you are doing", demanded an
unsuspecting policeman.

The King and Queen spent much of their time in London touring bombed
areas and giving comfort to those who had suffered in the raids. They narrowly
escaped disaster themselves when Buckingham Palace was hit by a bomb. "I'm
glad we have been bombed", Her Majesty said. "Now I can look the East Enders
in the face."

Many children from London's bombed areas became evacuees and were
sent into country areas for protection. Windsor was considered safe, and about
3,000 arrived during 1939. They were checked for health, labelled and, carrying
their gas-masks, sent to Bachelor's Acre where they were distributed among
hundreds of families in the district.

However, Windsor did become a target for German bombers. In September
1940 bombs fell on Alma Road, Goswell Road and Bridgewater Terrace. The
Germans returned in December and dropped hundreds of bombs in the Great
Park which did little damage. Some deaths, however, and many injuries

resulted from later raids. Local home defence groups were organised from centres in Victoria Street and Trinity Place, and the castle was protected by trenches and barbed wire fences. Years later Princess Margaret remarked that it would not have kept anybody out, "but it kept us in".

Eton also became a target for German bombers. Victorian windows were smashed when the college chapel was hit in 1940. Mr. Hill, an Eton teacher who also served six years on Eton Council, called it "a kindly bomb".

A plaque now adorns the house in Alma Road where Sidney Camm was born in 1893. He was educated at the Royal Free School, became fascinated by aircraft, and by the age of 18 had built a full-size glider. During the First World War he worked as an aircraft engineer, and in 1923 joined the Hawker Aircraft Company. Within two years he was the company's chief designer, leading a team which eventually built the Hurricane fighter, one of the most successful aircraft used in the war.

In May 1943, Duke of Kent and Princess Alexandra attended a Horse Show in the Home Park. With additional attractions of a circus, concerts, rabbit show, and a Grand Parade, the event was a huge success. This was the first of what is known today as the 'Royal Windsor Horse Show' which is very popular with the public.

159. Tractor and binder cutting oats in the Great Park while a farmer waits for rabbits to run out.

After the war, interest in the town's welfare led to another organisation being formed which still prospers, the 'Windsor & Eton Society'. This group was instituted at a meeting in the Guildhall in January 1946 with the aim of providing lectures and outings for its members, and to organise opposition against unwelcome development in the town. Sir Owen Morshead, Royal Librarian from 1926 to 1958, was mainly responsible for creating the body and became its first President.

For many years, Conservative councillors held power in the Guildhall and few considered that Labour stood any chance of altering the situation. But, as Raymond South, who has written a number of excellent books about Windsor, points out, the town has long had a radical streak. In 1945, following the national trend, Labour did sweep to victory in Windsor. They won the two Clewer Wards outright and made deep inroads in other divisions. They ended the day with 17 Labour to 23 Conservative representatives on the Council. A few months later, as a result of by-elections, Labour won four more seats. This gave them a majority of 21 to 19 and control in the Town Hall.

160. By 1945 the trees which lined the Long Walk had become so badly diseased they had to be cut down.

161. Mainly horse chestnut were planted as replacements.

However, it proved to be a short-lived victory. In elections the following year the Conservatives won all ten seats being contested, three of which had been held by Labour. But the surge in Labour support did result in Windsor's first Labour Mayor being elected. Fred Fuzzens held office for two-and-a-half years and represented the borough at the wedding of Princess Elizabeth and Prince Philip in Westminster Abbey in November 1947.

Mayor Fuzzens was in office during the severe floods which occurred that year. Heavy rain, which followed a severe winter, caused a catastrophe when deep frost prevented the land from soaking up the rain and melting snow. Sir Eric Savill described the water streaming through the Great Park as if it were "running off a slate roof". People had no warning as land at Wraysbury, Welley Road, Boveney and Dorney became flooded. Parts of Colnbrook High Street were soon 18 inches deep in water. Clewer church became an island as the water rose and flooded houses. Bungalows had to be evacuated; roads became impassable to cars and only useful as canals for boats; electric trains stopped running and steam trains found coal bunkers deep in water; telephones, gas, and electricity failed; shops sold out of candles and paraffin; food ran short and water became unfit to drink as sewers overflowed. Trees upriver, in danger of being uprooted by the water, had to be dynamited and removed to prevent them floating downstream and damaging Windsor Bridge. The swirling water caused the bridge to vibrate and shake as the torrent swept large boulders down the river. People worked day and night to assist flood victims and relieve the situation. When the floods did subside, they left behind a deposit of stinking mud which covered much of the town, as well as homes.

Windsor Bridge became so weak and over-burdened with traffic that eventually it became necessary to close it to motor traffic. Raymond South, who was active in furthering the plan, called it "a positive gain". It came about "almost accidentally ... ending a centuries-old link between Windsor and Eton". Consequently, Eton's High Street became comparatively tranquil as motor traffic was diverted to use a new bridge which formed part of a new bypass.

At the time, B. J. W. Hill was a member of Eton's Urban District Council. "Windsor is magnificent as an ancient Royal Borough", he wrote, "while Eton has a humble, but active Urban District Council, which meets in a disused fire station without pomp or ceremony." In 1957, his words recalled earlier problems when the two counties had argued over building the bridge at Datchet in George III's reign. "Eton designed a bypass, which ended opposite the most congested area of Windsor; the borough's planners placed their relief road half a mile upstream. Two years of negotiation were needed to make the roads meet on the map. Nevertheless, as in all other connections between Windsor and Eton, harmony is usually the keynote of relations between the two councils".

162. Windsor Bridge in 1989.

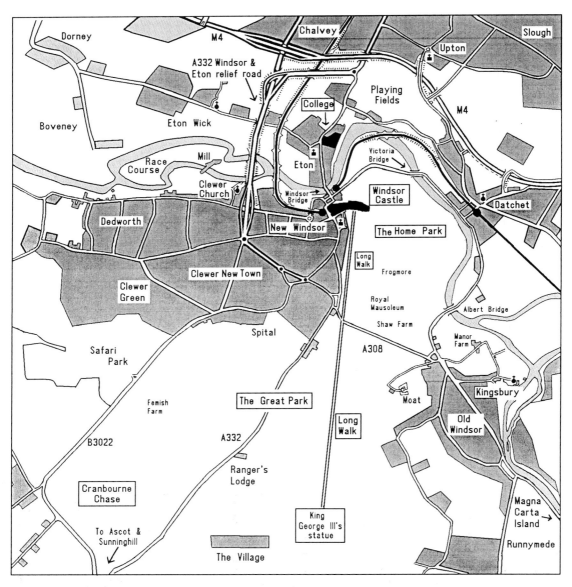

163. Windsor and district in 1990.

In 1974 a tremendous upheaval took place when the Government decided that the Royal Borough of Windsor was too small as an economical unit. It was part of a drastic scheme which changed boundaries throughout the country. Few people wanted the transformation and it was virtually forced through. As a result Windsor, with a population of 28,000, and Maidenhead with 49,000, were combined. The newly formed District Council received the title "Windsor and Maidenhead", and administration moved from Windsor's Guildhall to Maidenhead's Town Hall. Shortly afterwards, the new body was given the title "Royal Borough", but Windsor had lost much of its former independence.

It is surprising that a historic town like Windsor does not have its own museum — and this is not from want of trying by a number of people dedicated to preserving the borough's past for the future. In 1951 Maitland Underhill, Secretary of the Berkshire Archaeological Society, with the help of two enthusiastic supporters, Patrick Manley and Maurice Bond, established a museum in the Guildhall. Princess Elizabeth performed the opening ceremony on 15 May and young and old were attracted to see exhibits of the town's heritage. In 1982, following the local government reorganisation and lack of interest by the larger borough, the museum was forced to close. Another sad loss to the town followed when the its priceless records, which till then had been available to the public in the Guildhall and the Kipling Building, needed a suitable home. Such a building could not be found in Windsor and consequently all the old charters, deeds, accounts, and personal records were transferred to the safe keeping of Berkshire Records Office.

Raymond South wrote about housing development in 1977. "Estates, large and small, of private housing have been developed in several parts of the town, notably the 'Laing' estate to the west of Smith's Lane. Here are nearly a thousand houses and flats which extend over a large area where before were for the most part fields and open countryside. Most distinctive of the new housing is the controversial Ward Royal, controversial perhaps because of the monolithic fortress-like appearance it presents to the outside world, though composed of attractive flats and possessing many pleasant features. Completed in 1969, it gained a medal of diploma for good design in housing from the Ministry of Housing and Local Government. The query is rather whether, with its proximity to the town centre, it is right for its position."

Raymond South also highlighted problems which more than twelve years later have not been fully resolved. "Today Windsor is under pressure. Road and air traffic have dealt heavy blows at the town, assaulting its amenities and bringing into its life a highly unwelcome intrusion. The menace presented by jet aircraft was realised in the fifties, but at that time it was perhaps already too late ... it is difficult to envisage any worthwhile improvements in the foreseeable future. The road menace could have been foreseen and averted. Once the principle of an Eton by-pass had been accepted, however, the mismanaged 'Relief Road' was aimed straight at Windsor and the belt of open land between the eastern and western halves of the town offered planners a corridor which was too tempting to ignore. Whether the pattern of the motorways and the growth not only in the number but in the size of vehicles could have been foreseen is a matter of opinion. There is hope of alleviation when London's outer ring road — The North Orbital motorway — is completed ... "

In 1983, Maurice Bond was able to write optimistically about Windsor and the effect of the motorway system. "There has been much gain. The slums have at last gone. No 'inner-city blight' has resulted. The M4 and Heathrow have brought Windsor into the main current of international business life (one only needs to look at the brass name-plates, for instance, along Park Street). Windsor thus now is not just a castle accretion, or a London outer suburb. It has some light industry, a great deal of international finance and national headquarters for various societies. And of course, it still needs its hotels and shops for nearly

3 million annual tourists from all over the world."

With the accession of Her Majesty Queen Elizabeth, Windsor Castle again took on the role of Royal Palace and family home. The castle and borough continue a firm and happy relationship and the Town Hall is occasionally used for royal events. Her Majesty the Queen and other members of the royal family are active in supporting local organisations and can be seen at many public events. Her Majesty the Queen Mother frequently uses the Royal Lodge, and visits the town's theatre, often going back-stage to talk to players and staff. Andrew and Sarah, Duke and Duchess of York, have decided to make a home close to Windsor, in Sunninghill Park.

With so many targets for the IRA, security problems are immense. The army has to be on constant guard at the barracks, and the police remain vigilant in the streets. Retaining a balance between giving tourists access to the castle and keeping out terrorists creates constant problems for security staff. The Hundred Steps and the Round Tower, which offered a particularly tempting target or could be used as a vantage point for anyone wishing to snipe on those below, had to be closed.

Tourism remains the dominant factor, based on the castle. The atmosphere is that of a prosperous, pleasant community, with a good deal of local patriotism. But being a Windsor resident cannot be easy, even for those who profit from the trade. Winter and summer the streets can become blocked with cars, pavements are often turned into obstacle courses as they fill with visitors from *164. Tourists in the* all over the world, and prices in shops, cafés and pubs are frequently at a *Lower Ward.* premium.

Visitors arrive and are welcomed in their thousands, attracted by the unique experience of enjoying vast acres of parkland, beautiful gardens, a wildlife park, arts festivals, special exhibitions, sporting events, a majestic river offering boat trips to Maidenhead and Runnymede, a magnificent, living castle, and a thriving, pleasant town.

165. Peascod Street, leading up to Windsor Castle.

Bibliography

Ainsworth, W. Harrison, *Windsor Castle. An Historical Romance* (George Routledge and Sons, 1875).

Anonymous Diary (Norfolk Records Office, MS80 T 131 C).

Ashmole, Elias, *Order of the Garter* (1672/3).

Ballance, Selina, *A Town Called Eton* (Eton Press Ltd.).

Barlow, Frank, *Edward the Confessor* (Eyre Methuen Ltd., 1970).

Barrett, Charlotte, *Diary and Letters of Madame D'Arblay* (Swan Sonnenscheim & Co., 1893).

Benson, A. C. and Esher, Viscount, editors, *The Letters of Queen Victoria* (1908).

Billing's Directory (1854).

Bond, Maurice, The Story of Windsor (Local Heritage Books, 1984).

Bond, Shelagh, editor, *The First Hall Book of the Borough of New Windsor 1653-1725* (The Royal Borough of Windsor and Maidenhead Historical Records Publications, 1968).

Bowles, Rev. W., *History of Bremhill* (John Murray, 1823).

Carus, Dr. C. G., *The King of Saxoney's Journey Through England and Scotland* (Chapman and Hall, 1846).

Clemenson, Emily J. editor, *Passages from the Diaries of Mrs Phipip Lybbe Powyes* (Longman, Green, & Co., 1899).

Complete Traveller (1794).

Cobbett, William, *Rural Rides* (Reeves and Turner, 1908).

Cuthbert, Elizabeth H. editor, *The Sixth Hall Book of the Borough of New Windsor 1852-1874* (The Royal Borough of Windsor and Maidenhead Historical Records Publications, 1983).

Defoe, Daniel, *A Tour through the Whole Island of Great Britain* (The Folio Society, 1983).

Disbury, David G., *Berkshire in the Civil War* (1978).

Dixon, Hepworth, *Royal Windsor* (Hurst and Blackett, 4 vols., 1879/80).

Dutton's Directory (1863).

Elvey, Lady, *Life and Reminiscences of Sir George Elvey* (Sampson Low, 1894).

Erskine, Mrs. Stewart, editor, *Twenty Years at Court* (Nesbet & Co. 1916).

Evans, John, *An Excursion to Windsor* (Sherwood Gilbert and Piper, 1827).

Evelyn, John, *The Diary* (Macmillan and Co., Limited, 1906).

Falkner, John Meade, *Murray's Handbook for Berkshire* (Edward Stanford, 1902).

Goddard, Arthur, *Windsor, The Castle of Our Kings* (Jarrold & Sons, 1911/2).

Gransden, Antonia, *Historical Writing in England c. 440 to c. 1307* (Routledge & Kegan, 1974).

Greville, Charles C. F., *The Greville Memoirs* (8 vols. Longman, 1888).

Gruthuyse, Lord of, *Coming into Englande of the Lorde Grautehuse* (*Archaeologia*).

Hakewill, James, *The History of Windsor and its Neighbourhood* (Edmund Lloyd, 1813).

Harwood, T. Eustace, *Windsor Old and New* (Printed by Ballantyne Press for the Author, 1929).

Hedley, Olwen, *Round and About Windsor and District* (Oxley and Son, Windsor, 1948).

Hedley, Olwen, *Windsor Castle* (Robert Hale, 1967).

Helmlow, Joyce, editor, *Fanny Burney: Journals and Letters* (1973, BL X 0989/707).

Hentzer, Paul, *A Journey into England, in 1598* (Edited by Horace Walpole, Aungervyle Society, 1881).

Hibbert, Christopher, *The Court at Windsor: A Domestic History* (Longman, Green, & Co. Ltd., 1964).

Hill, B. J. W., *Windsor and Eton* (B. T. Batsford Limited, 1957).

Hill, M. D., *Eton and Elsewhere* (John Murray, 1928).

Holmes, R. R., *Windsor* (A. C. Blackie, 1908).

Hughes, G. M., *A History of Windsor Forest* (Ballantyne, Hanson & Co., 1890).

Hunt, *Royal Windsor Directory* (1846).

Hunter, J., *The Changing Face of Windsor: 1 — The Beginnings* (Windsor Local History Group, 1977).

Hunter, J. and Hedges, B., *Windsor Castle, Town and Park*.

Jesse, E., *Summers Day at Windsor* (John Murray, 1841).

Kelly's Directory: Berkshire (1887).

Knight, Charles (Senior), *Windsor Guide* (from 1793).

Knight, Charles (Senior), *Beauties of the Royal Palaces, and Gazetteer to the Towns, Villages, Villas, and Remarkable Places within Sixteen Miles of Windsor* (1798).

Knight, Charles (Junior), *Passages of a Working Life* (Bradbury Evans, 1864).

Knight, Cornelia, *Autobiography of Miss Cornelia Knight, Lady Companion to the Princess Charlotte of Wales* (W. H. Allen, 1861).

Langton, Jane, editor, *Second Hall Book of the Borough of New Windsor 1726-1783* (The Royal Borough of Windsor and Maidenhead Historical Publications, 1973).

Lawrence P. S. H., *An Eton Camera 1850-1919* (Michael Russell, 1980).

Lee, Albert, *The Story of Royal Windsor* (Jarrold and Sons).

Loftie, W. J., *Windsor, A Description of the Castle, Park, Town and Neighbourhood* (1886).

Luttrel, Narcissus, *Relation of State Affairs 1678 - 1714* (6 vols. Oxford University Press, 1857).

Lysons, Daniel and Samuel, *Magna Britannia* (Cadell, 1806).

Lyttelton, Lady, *Correspondence of Sarah Spencer, Lady Lyttelton* (John Murray, 1912).

Macky, John, *Journies Through England* (J. Roberts for T. Caldecott, 1714).

Macnaghten, Angus, *Windsor in Georgian Times* (Luff and Co., 1976).

Macnaghten, Angus, *Windsor in Victorian Times* (Luff and Co., 1975).

Measom, George, *Guide to the Great Western Railway* (Marshall & Sons, 1852).

Menzies, William, *Windsor Park and Forest* (Oxley and Sons, 1904).

Morris, Chistopher, editor, *The Illustrated Journeys of Celia Fiennes* (Webb & Bower, 1988).

Morshead, Sir Owen, *Windsor Castle* (Phaidon Press, 1951).

Murray, John, *Handbook For Travellers* (John Murray, 1882).

Nichols, John, *The Progress and Public Processions of Elizabeth* (5 vols. Society of Antiquaries, 1788-1821).

Nichols, John, *Progress of James the First* (4 vols. Society of Antiquaries, 1828).

Page, W. & Rev P. H. Ditchfield, *Victoria History of the County of Berkshire* (University of London, 1923).

Pevsner, Nikolaus, *The Buildings of England – Berkshire* (Penguin Books, 1966).

Pinkerton, John, *Voyages and Travels* (Longman, Hurst, Rees and Orme, 1808).

Platter, Thomas, *Travels in England 1599* (translated by C. Williams, 1937).

Ponsonby, Frederick, *Recollections of Three Reigns* (Eyre & Spottiswoode, 1951).

Pote, J., *History and Antiquities of Windsor* (Joseph Pote, 1749).

Pote, T. & J., *Les Delices de Windsor or a description of Windsor Castle* (Guide Book, 1755).

Pratt, Rev. Josiah, *The Acts and Monuments of John Foxe* (Religious Tract Society, 1877).

Ritchie, L., *Windsor Castle and its Environs* (Longmans, 1840).

Rowse, A. L., *Windsor Castle in the History of the Nation* (Weidenfeld & Nicolson, 1974).

Rye, W. B., *England as seen by Foreigners* (John Russel Smith, 1865).

Scott Thomson, Gladys, editor, *Letters of a Grandmother 1732-1735* (Jonathan Cape, 1943).

St. John Hope, W. H., *Windsor Castle, Architectural History* (2 vols. Country Life, 1913).

South, R., *The Book of Windsor* (Barracuda, 1977).

South, R., *Crown, College and Railways* (Barracuda, 1978).

South, R., *Royal Castle, Rebel Town* (Barracuda, 1981).

South, R, editor, *The Fifth Hall Book of the Borough of New Windsor 1828-1852* (The Royal Borough of Windsor and Maidenhead Historical Records Publications, 1974).

Stanley, Lady Augusta, *Letters of Lady Augusta Stanley* (Gerald Howe Ltd., 1927).

Swift, Jonathan, edited by Harold Williams, *Journals to Stella* (Oxford at the Clarendon Press, 1948).

Tighe, R. R. and Davis, J. E. *Annals of Windsor* (Longman, Brown, Green, Longmans and Roberts, 1858).

Trevisano, Andrea, *A Relation of England* (translated by C. A. Sneyd. Camden Society, 1847).

Triphook, Robert, 'Diary' (Norfolk Records Office, DS 622 P 137 C).

Trom, Heimerick, *Dutchman's Visits to some English Gardens in 1791* (Journal of Garden History).

Tucker, W. H., *Eton of Old or Eighty Years Since 1811 - 1822* (Griffith Farran & Co., 1892).

Universal Directory of British Trade (1796).

Vincent, James, *Highways and Byways in Berkshire* (Macmillan, 1906).

Walford, Edward, *Tourist's Guide To Berkshire* (Edward Stanford, 1882).

Watson, Vera, *A Queen at Home* (W. H. Allen, 1952).

Wheatley, Henry B., *The Diary of Samuel Pepys* (George Bell & Sons, 1895).

Williams, Clare, editor, *Thomas Platter's Travels in England in 1599* (Jonathan Cape, 1937).

Williams, Harold, *see* Swift, Jonathan.

Wilson, David Gordon, *The Making of the Middle Thames* (Spurbooks Ltd., 1977).

Woodham-Smith, C., *Queen Victoria 1819-61* (1972).

Windlesora (Journal of the Windsor Local History Publications Group).

Index

Abingdon, 28, 40
Adelaide, Queen, 78
Adeliza of Louvain, 6
Agers, John, 51
Albert Institute, 103
Albert Institute Operatic & Dramatic Society, 108
Albert Memorial Chapel, 93
Albert, Prince, 92-93, 95, 98
aldermen, 35, 78, 92
Alexandra, Princess, 113
Alexandra, Queen, 95
Alfred, King, 4
All Saints' Church, 103
Alma Road, 112-113
Amelia, Princess, 71
Andrews, John, 57
Anne, Queen, 54, 56-58
Anne, Queen (James I), 35
Antelope, 35
Argand, Professor, 67
Ascham, Roger, 29
Ascot, 56, 103, 110
Augusta, Princess, 71

Bachelor's Acre, 70, 72, 102, 112
Bagshaw, Mr., 39
Bagshot, 28, 41, 84
Bagshot Heath, 86
bailiffs, 9-12, 58
barracks, 44, 64, 71, 102, 110-111
Bath, 59, 67
baths, 22, 31, 32
Battenberg, Prince Louis of, 95
Bay Heath, 84
Beauchamp, Richard, 23
Beckeley, John, 18
Bell, Alexander Graham, 104
Bells of Ouzeley, 85, 97
Bennet, Robert, 27
Berkhampstead, 6
Berkshire Records Office, 117
Bier Lane, 93
Biljoen, Baron, 69
Binfield, 84
Bishopsgate Street, 51
black death, 13
Blackmore Park, 30
Blacks, The, 59
Blackwater, 84
Blues, 70-71
Board of Health, 102

Bond, Maurice, 117
Boughton, 18
Boveney, 1, 10, 115
Bowles, Rev. W., 76
Boleyn, Anne, 25-26, 32
Boy Scouts, 106
Bracknell, 86
bridges, 11, 19, 25-26, 28, 47, 53, 55, 57-58, 61, 66, 68, 73, 100, 104, 109, 115
Bridgewater Terrace, 112
Bridgewater, Earl of, 56
Brighton Pavilion, 77
Bristol, 7, 97
Brixham, 55
Bronze Age, 2
brothels, 102
Brown, Henry, 93
Brown, J. B., 66
Browning, Capt. Charles Hunter, 111
Brunel, Isambard Kingdom, 98
Buckeridge, citizen, 37
Buckingham Palace, 63, 66, 77, 112
bull baiting, 64, 70, 82
burgesses, 92
Burgundy, 22
Burney, Fanny, 65, 68-69
Burnham, 13
Burnham, Cugina de, 10
Burnside, Mr., 100

Caffyn's Corner, 108
Calais, 13, 17, 26
Caly's store, 108
Cambridge, 18, 21, 79
Camm, Sidney, 113
Canon John, 14
Canons, 25, 27, 39, 103
Canons' Cloisters, 25
Canterbury, 4
Canterbury, Archbishop of, 6, 111
Cardinal's Hat, 35
Carlton House, 77
Carlton, Sir Dudley, 35
Carus, Dr., 98, 100, 103
Castle Hill, 51, 66, 95-96, 105
Castle Hotel, 71
Catherine of Aragon, 24-26
Catherine of France, 17
Catholic Church, 54-55, 103
Caversham, 43
Cedars, The, 106

Chalvey, Christina de, 10
Chamberlain, Lord, 22
Channel Islands, 17
Chapman, John, 73
Charles I, 38-43
Charles II, 44-45, 49-50, 54, 60, 76, 102
Charles, Thomas, 49
Charlotte, Queen, 63, 65, 67, 70, 73
Chertsey Abbey, 21
Chinese Temple, 85
Chirmild, Thomas, 38
cholera, 93
Christian, Prince, 96
Christian, Princess, 109
Christopher Inn, 64, 81, 84
Church Street, 106
cinemas, 108
Civil Guard, 110
Civil War, 40, 42-44, 46, 49
Clarendon, Lord, 40
Clewer, 1, 5, 10, 88, 97, 99, 102-103, 110, 113, 115
Clewer Horticultural Society, 110
Clewer Lane, 102
Clewer volunteers, 70
Clode, William, 97
clubs, 109
coaches, 51, 54, 57, 59, 92, 97
Cobbett, William, 85
Cobham, 18
Colnbrook, 25, 97, 115
Commonwealth, 43-44
Compton, Sir Francis, 59
Conservatives, 113
Constables, 9-11, 17, 49, 58
Cooper, Mrs., 55
Copper Horse, 74, 78
Corbett, Mr., 78
Corn Exchange, 111
Corporation, 27, 44, 46, 55, 57, 64, 66, 71, 78, 94, 99, 102, 104, 109
Cotterel, Sir George, 54
councillors, 9, 12, 37, 44, 50, 52, 56, 92, 101, 109, 113
Cranborne Chase, 35
Craven, Lord, 43
Crécy, 13
Cromwell, Oliver, 40, 43
Cross Keys, 35
Crown, 35, 98
Cumberland, 6
Cumberland Lodge, 92
Cumberland, Duke of, 86
Curfew Tower, 6, 26, 46, 51, 55, 64
Cygony, Engelard de, 9

D'Adda, Monsignor, 54
Danegeld, 4
Dartford, 14
Datchet, 1, 15, 25, 45, 56-57, 61, 66, 68, 115
David, King of Scotland, 14
Dean, John, 28
Deans, 25, 46, 49, 57, 92
Dedworth, 1

Defoe, Daniel, 30, 60
Denmark, George, Prince of, 56-57
Devereux, Robert, Earl of Essex, 40
dispensary, 73
Disraeli, 94
Djebelia, 110
Dorney, 1, 115
Dragoons, 40
Draper, Hugh the, 9
Dreux, Robert de, 7
ducking stool, 28
Durham, 14
Dutch navy, 55
Dutton's Directory, 103
Duval, Mrs., 70

Easthampstead, 18
Edward I, 8, 11-12
Edward II, 12
Edward III, 11, 13, 15
Edward III's Tower, 45
Edward IV, 20, 23
Edward VI, 32
Edward VII, 91, 94-95, 101, 103
Edward VIII [Duke of Windsor], 112
Edward the Confessor, 4-5, 8, 103
Edward, Prince, 19, 21
Edward, Prince of York, 95
Edwards, Elizabeth, 58
Egham, 97
Eglestone, Mr., 78
Eleanor, Queen, 8, 13
electricity, 104, 115
Elizabeth I, 26, 29, 32, 34-35
Elizabeth II, 24, 69, 112, 115, 117-118
Elizabeth, Princess, 66, 71
Elizabeth, Queen Mother, 118
Ellison, Canon, 103
Ethelred, King, 4
Eton, 1, 9, 25, 32, 57, 64-65, 70-71, 73, 80, 84, 92, 94, 99-100, 104, 108-109, 113, 115, 117
Eton College, 17-21, 25, 50, 53, 69, 79, 82, 93-94, 98, 106
Eton Wick, 2
Eton, Warde Close, 19
evacuees, 112
Evans, John, 71
Evelyn, John, 43, 47-49
Exeter, 55

Fairfax, Sir Thomas, 40
fairs, 15, 46, 82
farming, 69, 85, 92, 106
Fiennes, Celia, 53
Fifth Infantry, 85
Filmer, Henry, 27
Fire Brigade, 78
fires, 4, 52, 78
fisheries, 1, 10, 19
Fitz, Sir Thomas, 52
Fitz Hugh, John, 9
Fitz Walter, William, 9

floods, 6, 13, 28, 81, 86, 97, 102-103, 115
Fogg, Captain, 23
Foliejon Park, 18
Ford, Mr., 78
Forest Ranger, 11, 86
Franklyn's almshouses, 34
Free School, 57, 113
Frith, Mr., 28
Frogmore, 61, 70, 72, 92, 94-96
Frogmore Green, 84
Fuzzens, Fred, 115

Gaimer's chronicle, 4
Galland, Mr., 44
Galloway's, 84
gallows, 26, 28
gaols, 6, 12, 41, 44
Gardener, Robert the, 9
gardens, 22, 31, 47, 56, 68, 70, 84, 87, 91-92, 119
Garter Ceremony, 13, 23-25, 46, 48
Garter Inn, 28, 35-36
gas, 78, 115
gateways, 9, 15, 24, 26-27, 39, 51, 64, 71, 75, 106, 109
Gentleman's Magazine, 64
George I, 58
George II, 58, 86
George III, 63, 65-67, 69-72, 74, 76, 101-102
George IV, 43, 48, 63, 71, 74, 76, 89
George V, 87, 106, 110-111
George VI, 112
George, The, 35
George Street, 100
Germans, 110-113
gibbet, 28
Gibbons, Grinling, 49
Girl Guides, 112
Glaziers Corner, 64
Gloucester, Bishop of, 39
Gloucester, Duchess of, 89
Gloucester, Duke of, 56
Glover, James, 9-10
Goodman, Dr. Godfrey, 39
Goring, widow, 28
Goswell Road, 112
Grafton, Duke of, 54
Gravesend, 41
Greenwich, 24
Greville, Charles, 68, 74, 77
Grythuyse, Lord, 22
Guards, 71, 85, 108, 111
guild of merchants, 12
Guildford, 6
Guildhall, 36, 52-53, 56-57, 71, 73-74, 78, 113, 117

Halford, Sir Henry, 43
Ham Island, 102
Hammersley's maid, 28
Hampton Court, 56
Harold, King, 5
Harpesford, 86
Harris, Windsor attorney, 28
Hastings, 5

Hatfield House, 29
Hawtrey, Dame, 81
hearth tax, 45
Helena Day, 110
Henley-on-Thames, 67
Henry I, 6, 10, 17, 63
Henry II, 6
Henry III, 8-11
Henry VI, 13, 17-21, 32, 98
Henry VII, 23, 25, 32
Henry VIII, 24-27, 32, 42-43
Hentzner, Paul, 32, 50
Herbert's store, 108
Herbert, servant, 42
heretics, 18
Herne's Oak, 35, 101
Herschel, William, 67
Hertford, 6
Hertford, Marquis of, 42
High Church, 39
High Steward of Windsor, 96
High Street, 74, 99, 104
highwaymen, 59
Hill, B. J. W., 76, 113, 115
Holland, Lord, 39
Hollis, Charles, 73
Holy Trinity Church, 103
Hope Inn, 84
horse races, 45, 56, 103, 110
Horton, 1
House of Commons, 39, 41, 75
House of Lords, 39-40
House of Mercy, 102
Hull, 40
Hundred Steps, 31, 35, 92, 101, 118
Hungerford Bridge, 83
hunting, 5, 10-11, 22, 25, 34-35, 37, 49, 56, 70, 84
Husteds, Mr., 104
Hyde, Anne, 54

Ice Ages, 2
Illustrated London News, 102
inns, 18, 23, 28-29, 32, 34, 40, 46, 52, 64-65, 71, 101-102, 105

James I, 35, 37
James II, 46, 54-55, 67, 70
Jesse, Edward, 99
Jews, 10
Joan of Arc, 17
John, King, 6-7
Jones, Francis, 39
Jones, William, 73

Keat's Chambers, 81
Keep, see Round Tower
Kelly's Directory, 103
Kent, Duke of, 113
Kent, Nathaniel, 69
Kent, Victoria, Duchess of, 89
Keppel, Admiral, 65
Kew, 68
King Edward VII's Hospital, 110

Kipling Building, 117
Kitchener, Lord, 111
Knight, Charles, 64, 66-67, 70, 72, 74, 80, 97
Knight, Cornelia, 70
Knights Companion, 23-24, 46, 111
Knights, poor, 31, 46

Labour, party, 113
Lancashire Volunteers, 64
Lancastrians, 19-21
land enclosure, 85
Lee, Albert, 105
Leopold I, King of the Belgians, 92
Limes, The, 102
Lindesay, William de, 14
Liverpool, Lord, 75
Locke, Joseph, 98
Locker, Edward Hawke, 73
Loddon river, 4, 10
London, 3-7, 14, 19, 26-29, 50, 53, 57-59, 67, 71, 85,
    94, 97-99, 105, 110-112, 117
London Gazette, 50-51
London, Bishop of, 42
London, Dr., 27
Long Chamber, 81
Long Walk, 49, 61, 63-64, 71, 74-76, 78, 92, 95, 99, 110,
    114
Lord High Treasurer, 57
Losfield, 1
Louis Philippe, King of France, 92, 98
Louis, Prince (VIII), 7
Lower Ward, 14, 24-26, 31, 90
Luttrel, Narcissus, 45, 52, 55-56

Macky, John, 60
Maclean, Mr., 100
Magna Carta, 7
Maidenhead, 116, 119
Maidenhead Thicket, 59
Maids' Acre, 73
Maidstone, 18
Manley, Patrick, 117
marathon, 110
Marbeck, John, 27
Margaret of Anjou, 19-21
Margaret, Princess, 112
Market Cross, 53
Market Hall, 36
Market House, 34, 38
Marlborough, Sarah, Duchess of, 83
Marlow, Little, 18
Martin, John, 37
martyrs, 27
Mary Beatrice of Modena, 54-55
Mary I, 25-26, 29
Mary II, 54, 56, 60
Mary, Queen (George V), 106
Mausoleum, 95
May, Hugh, 47
May, Princess, 96
Mayors, 12, 35, 37-39, 44, 50, 53, 57-58, 64, 72, 92, 94,
    108-111, 115

maypole, 44
Mercia, 3
Michener, Richard, 38
mills, 1, 3, 13, 46, 88
Monsell, Harriet, 102
Moor Street, 34, 38
Moore, John, 73
Moore, William, 73
Moritz, Charles P., 64-65, 79
Morland, Samuel, 50
Morshead, Sir Owen, 76, 113
Morton, Colonel, 56
Murray, John, 105-106
Murray's Handbook, 75, 101
museum, 103, 117

Napoleon III, 92
National School, 73
Nell Gwynne, 47, 56, 102
Neolithic pottery, 2
Nevers, Count, 7
Nevill, Hugh de, 9
New Lodge, 39
Newark, 18
Newbury, 27-28
Newman, Mr., 45
Nicholas I, Emperor of Russia, 92
Norden, John, 35-36
Norfolk, Duke of, 26, 58
North Star, 98
Northampton, 19

O'Reilly, John, 73
Old Wells Inn, 83
Old Windsor, 1-4, 6, 9, 28, 49, 59, 61, 102
Orton, 1
Osborne, 95
Owen, Henry, 112
Oxford, 18, 40, 55

Paddington, 98
parish church, 10, 16, 44-45, 74, 103, 106
Park School, 112
Park Street, 34, 117
parks, 10-12, 15, 22, 25, 28, 32, 34-35, 45, 49, 56, 60,
    63, 66, 69, 74, 84-86, 101, 109, 112-113, 115, 119
Pearson, Anthony, 27
Peascod Street, 24, 35, 44, 104-106
Pelham-Clinton, Lord Edward, 96
Pembroke, Earl of, 55
Penington, Mr., 57
Pepys, Samuel, 46, 79
Perres, Alice, 15
Perres, Isabella, 15
Perry, Mr., 101
pest house, 38
Pevsner, Nikolaus, 105
Pewke, Reginald, 18
Philip, King of Castile, 23
Philip, Prince, 115
Philip-Augustus, 7
Philippa, Queen, 15
Pilgrimage of Grace, 26

pillory, 27-28, 36
plagues, 13, 29, 38, 50
Platter, Thomas, 32
Plymouth, 24
poaching, 11, 37
Poitiers, 13
Pontefract, 20
poor, 45-46, 72-73, 93, 102-103
Portsmouth, Duchess of, 60
post service, 51, 106
Pound Street, 38
Powys, Mrs. Philip Lybbe, 66
Poynter,Ambrose, 49
Printer, Roger, 28
prisoners, 12
Private Apartments, 101
Protestant Church, 27, 54-55
Prussia, Victoria, Crown Princess of, 103
Pycheford, Geoffrey de, 10

Quadrangle, see Upper Ward
Queen's Lodge, 63, 68, 76

railways, 95, 97-101, 105, 109, 111
Ralf, son of Seifride, 5
Ramsbottom's brewery, 78
Ramsey Abbey, 4
Randue, Theodore, 57
Reading, 4, 10-12, 27-28, 40, 43, 55, 59
Red Cross, 110
Rendall, William, 73
Richard I, 10
Richbell, citizen, 37
Richmond, 55
Richmond Palace, 35
Richmond, Duke of, 42
rioting, 37, 39, 41, 64
River Street, 93
roads, 97, 100, 109, 117
Rochester, 6
Romans, 3
Rose, 35
Round Tower, 8, 14, 31-32, 49-50, 58, 74-76, 95
Rowse, A. L., 76
Royal Lodge, 74, 89, 112, 118
Royal School, 92
Royal stables, 82
Royal Windsor Horse Show, 113
Runnymede, 2, 7, 119
Rupert, Prince, 40, 49, 52
Rustat, Tobias, 49, 76

Saddler, widow, 9
St Albans, Duke of, 102
St George's Chapel, 14, 21, 23, 25, 27, 29, 31, 40,
    42-43, 46, 57, 67, 77, 91-92, 94-95, 111
St George's College, 13
St George's Hall, 31, 48, 75
St James Palace, 55
St Paul's, 19
St Peter's Hospital, 10
St Saviour's Chapel, 103
Salisbury, Bishop of, 6, 23

Sandby, Paul, 86
Sandby, Thomas, 86
Sandwich, 7
Savill Gardens, 87
Savill, Sir Eric, 87, 115
Saxons, 1, 4-5, 10, 15
Saxony, King of, 98
Scotland, 20
Sea Rangers, 112
Seymour, Jane, 26-27, 42
Shakespeare, William, 32
Sheet Street, 38, 64, 78, 102-103
Sherwell, Thomas, 38
Ship Hotel, 106
Silchester, 3
Simonds, William, 27
Siward, Richard, 11
Skinner, Karina, 73
Slough, 18, 79, 98-100, 109
slums, 102, 117
Smith, John, 18
Smith, Simon, 49
Smith's Lane, 117
Snow Hill, 74, 78
Snowden, Philip, 109
Sopwith, Thomas, 106
South, Raymond, 113, 115, 117
Southampton, Earl of, 46
Spanish Armada, 24
Spital Road, 102
Stads, Josias, 49
Staffords, 70
Staines, 2-3, 5, 84
Stamfordham, Lord, 111
Starithe, Gilbert de, 11
Starithe, John de, 11
State Apartments, 47, 108-109
Stewart, Dr., 73
stocks, 28
Stow, John, 29, 31
suffragettes, 108-109, 111
Sunninghill, 18, 83-85, 118
Surveyor, Deputy, 87
Swan, 73
sweeps, 72
Swift, Jonathan, 56
Swinley Lodge, 84

Taylor, Joseph, 104
Tennant, Mrs., 102
Terrace, 30, 50, 67-71, 74, 94, 101
Territorials, 106
Testwood, Robert, 27
Tewkesbury, 21
Thames river, 1, 3-5, 8, 21, 51, 55, 57, 60, 64, 67, 73,
    81, 86, 93, 97, 99-100, 103, 115
Thames Street, 25, 36, 58, 64, 69, 78, 92, 94, 99, 104
Thames Valley, 2
Theatre, 69, 108, 118
Thumwood's coach, 81
Tighe and Davis, 14, 49, 51, 67, 82, 86, 92
Times newspaper, 94

Tonbridge, 83
tournaments, 12-13
Tower of London, 6, 14, 26
Town Hall, 44, 50, 52, 70, 82, 99, 105-106, 108, 110-111, 118
Towton, 20
Travers, Mr., 58
Treaty of Windsor, 24
Trevisano, Andrea, 34
Trigge, Mr., 73
Trinity Place, 103, 113
Triphook, Richard, 83
troops, 37, 39-41, 44, 46, 59, 64, 70-71, 85, 95, 99, 102, 108, 110-111
Tucker, Mr., 79, 81-82
Tyburn, 59
typhoid, 93

Umberfield, Edward, 28
Underhill, Maitland, 117
Universal Directory of British Trade, 83
Upper Ward, 14, 31, 47, 49, 67, 70, 75-76, 90, 95
Upton, 1, 25, 67

Venn, Colonel, 40
Verrio, Antonio, 47-49, 54, 75
Vicarage, 106
Vicars, 37, 57, 110
Victor Emmanuel, King of Sardinia, 92
Victoria Street, 113
Victoria, Queen, 89, 92-96, 98, 100-104
Vikings, 4
Vincent, James Edmund, 101, 105
Virginia Water, 84, 86, 89
visitors, 24, 29, 31-32, 34, 60, 64, 68, 71, 84, 100-101, 103, 108, 118

Wakefield, 19
Walford, Edward, 86, 101
Wallingford, 12, 55
Walpole, Horace, 50, 65
Walstein, Baron , 32
Ward Royal, 117
Wargrave, 109
Wars of the Roses, 19-20
water supply, 3, 8, 30-31, 38, 50, 92, 115
Waterloo, 71, 85
Watkins, Thomas, 28
Waynflete, William, 19
Webb, Godfrey, 28
Welley Road, 115
Wellington, Duke of, 71, 77
wells, 8, 38, 83
Wesleyan community, 108
Wessex, 3-4
Westbury, William, 20
Westerly, Robert, 18
Westminster, 14, 23, 41, 94, 106
Westminster Abbey, 4, 17, 20, 115
Weston's Yard, 81
wharf, 23
Wheteley, Robert, 18

whipping post, 28
Whistley, 4
White Hart, 35-36, 97, 101, 104-105
Wikes, John, 37
wildlife park, 119
Wilkins, Mrs., 55
William II, Prince of Orange, 50
William III, 54-56
William IV, 86, 89
William the Conqueror, 1, 5, 10, 17
Willows, The, 109
Wilton, 55
Winchester, 4, 18-19, 24
Winchester, Bishop of, 96
Winchester, Marquis of, 29
Windsor:
    and Eton Literary Institute, 78; and Maidenhead District Council, 116; attacked, 7, 40; Borough, 12-13, 19, 34, 38, 44, 57-58, 74, 78, 111, 115-116, 118; Castle, 1, 5-7, 9, 13-14, 24-25, 29-31, 43, 47, 49, 58, 60, 62, 66-67, 74-75, 78, 89-90, 112, 118 chapel, 8, 13-14; Cross, 15, 39, 44; development of, 9, 15, 34, 44-45, 58, 63, 66, 105-106, 117; *Express* newspaper, 69, 72, 78, 99, 108-110; Forest, 1, 6, 10-11, 35, 37, 39, 45, 52, 59-60, 83-84, 86, 101; Horticultural Society, 78; House of, 111; improvements to castle, 8, 13, 23, 30, 47, 49, 70, 74; market, 10, 13, 15, 23, 27-28, 35, 38, 46; Royal Society, 92
Windsor & Eton Society, 113
Windsor, Ivo of, 10
Windsor, Maurice of, 10
Windsor, Richard of, 10
Windsor, William of, 10
wine, 6, 19, 35
Winkfield, 30, 92
Winkfield Park, 84
Wirtemburg, Duke of, 29, 31, 34
Wokingham, 85
Wolf Hall, 26
Wolsey's chapel, 25, 40, 54, 67, 70, 93
Wolsey, Cardinal, 25, 40, 54
World War, First, 110-111, 113
World War, Second, 87, 112
Wraysbury, 1-2, 115
Wren, Christopher, 57
Wren, Sir Christopher, 49, 52
Wyatt, James, 70
Wyatville, Sir Jeffry, 75
Wycliffe, John, 18

York, 20, 39
York, Andrew, Duke of, 118
York, Archbishop of, 25
York, Frederick, Duke of, 68
York, Richard, Duke of, 19
York, Sarah, Duchess of, 118
York Minster, 19
Yorkists, 20-21